MW01077718

The Majority Press

THE JEWISH ONSLAUGHT:
Despatches from the Wellesley Battlefront

TONY MARTIN has taught at Wellesley College, Massachusetts since 1973. He was tenured in 1975 and has been a full professor of Africana Studies since 1979. Prior to coming to Wellesley he taught at the University of Michigan-Flint, the Cipriani Labour College (Trinidad) and St. Mary's College (Trinidad). He has been a visiting professor at the University of Minnesota, Brandeis University, Brown University and The Colorado College. He also spent a year as an honorary research fellow at the University of the West Indies, Trinidad.

Professor Martin has authored or compiled and edited eleven books, including *Literary Garveyism: Garvey, Black Arts and the Harlem Renaissance* and the classic study of the Garvey Movement, *Race First: the Ideological and Organizational Struggles of Marcus Garvey and the Universal Negro Improvement Association*. He qualified as a barrister-at-law at the Honourable Society of Gray's Inn (London) in 1965, did a B.Sc. honours degree in economics at the University of Hull (England) and the M.A. and Ph.D. in history at Michigan State University.

Professor Martin is currently working on biographies of three Caribbean women – Amy Ashwood Garvey, Audrey Jeffers and Trinidad's Kathleen Davis ("Auntie Kay"). He is also nearing completion of *The Afro-Trinidadian: Endangered Species/Oh, What a Nation* and a study of European Jewish immigration to Trinidad in the 1930's.

Other Books By Tony Martin

Literary Garveyism: Garvey, Black Arts
and the Harlem Renaissance

The Poetical Works of Marcus Garvey

Marcus Garvey, Hero: A First Biography

African Fundamentalism: A Literary Anthology of
Garvey's Harlem Renaissance

The Pan-African Connection: From Slavery to Garvey and Beyond

Message to the People: The Course of African Philosophy
(By Marcus Garvey. Ed. by Tony Martin)

Race First: the Ideological and Organizational Struggles of Marcus
Garvey and the Universal Negro Improvement Association

In Nobody's Backyard: the Grenada Revolution in its Own Words
(Two Volumes)

Rare Afro-Americana: A Reconstruction of the Adger Library
(with Wendy Ball)

THE JEWISH ONSLAUGHT

Despatches from the Wellesley Battlefront

Tony Martin

THE MAJORITY PRESS
Dover, Massachusetts

Library of Congress Cataloging in Publication Data

Martin, Tony, 1942-
        The Jewish Onslaught: despatches from the Wellesley battlefront / Tony Martin.
                    p. cm.
            Includes index.
            ISBN 0-912469-30-7 (paper) : $9.95
        1.   Afro-Americans--Relations with Jews.   2. Secret relationship between Blacks and Jews. 3. Wellesley College. I. Title.
    E185.615.M3 1993
    380.1'44'08996--dc20   93-36512
                                                          CIP

First published in 1993

10 9 8 7 6 5 4 3 2

The Majority Press
P.O. Box 538
Dover, Massachusetts 02030

Printed in the United States of America

Contents

The African Nationalist Construction Movement &
Patrice Lumumba Coalition
in Association with the Universal Negro Improvement Association
and African Communities League
are Issuing a Call for an African Community Forum on

ACADEMIC FREEDOM AND THE RIGHT
TO TELL THE HISTORICAL TRUTH
A RALLY IN DEFENSE OF
DR. TONY MARTIN

Wellesley College, Massachusetts
Author of **RACE FIRST** - The Ideological and Organizational Struggles
of Marcus Garvey and the Universal Negro Improvement Association
20 Year Tenured Professor of Africana Studies

FRIDAY, MAY 14TH, 1993
6:30 p.m. until 10 p.m.
HARRIET TUBMAN SCHOOL
127th Street & Adam Clayton Powell, Jr. Boulevard

Invited Guest Speakers

DR. JOHN HENRIK CLARKE
African Historian Emeritus
MARCUS GARVEY, JR.
UNIA & ACL
SAMORI MARKSMAN
Dir. African & Caribbean Resource Center

DR. LEONARD JEFFRIES
CCNY Black Studies Dept.
VIOLA PLUMMER
December 12th Movement
ELOMBE BRATH
Patrice Lumumba Coalition

ROBERT ACEMENDESES HARRIS
African Nationalist Construction Movement

Also Representatives from the Nation of Islam Historical Research Dept.
All-African People's Revolutionary Party and Others

Donations: $3.00 Further Information, call (212)663-3805/9 (212)666-3800

SAVE MUMIA ABU JAMAL - KEEP DHORUBA FREE

Preface

In January 1993, on the eve of the Jewish onslaught against me (for teaching that Jews were implicated in the African slave trade), I already had some interest in Black-Jewish relations. It is difficult not to, if one teaches African American history. I had also done some research on Jewish refugee immigration to Trinidad in the 1930's and '40's. This research was facilitated by the cordial cooperation of Jewish informants in two Caribbean countries. United States Jews encountered in the course of the research displayed the gamut of reactions, from friendliness to suspicion to hostility. The idea of a Black man turning up at a Jewish archive to research Jewish history proved unnerving to some. (On the other hand, Jewish scholars are a familiar sight at Black archives, not only as researchers but sometimes even as staff archivists. One of the most prestigious of the Black archival repositories, the Moorland-Spingarn Collection of Howard University, is actually part-named after a Jew).

At one of the Jewish archives I visited, the lady in charge characteristically put me through the appropriate litmus test. "Do you know Len Jeffries?" she asked, with the mien of one presiding over an inquisition. "I wonder if knowing Len Jeffries automatically disqualifies me from using these archives," I mused to myself. But, like George Washington, I could not tell a lie, so I was constrained to be forthcoming. "Yes, I know him," I replied. "We are professional colleagues. I have known him for many years." She was visibly taken aback by this answer and I feared the worst.

She regained her composure, however, and the interrogation continued. "Have you read *The Secret Relationship Between Blacks and Jews*?" "I have heard of it," I replied truthfully, "but I have not read it. Funny enough, though, I passed someone selling it on the sidewalk just a few minutes ago." My reading of the book was still a few months into the future, but already I could not fathom what all the fuss was about. "If it is established," I suggested to her, "that white people enslaved Africans, and if Jews were an important part of white society, then why should anyone be upset by a book that illustrates the Jewish role in the slave trade?"

My innocent question now appears to have been imbued with prophetic insight. Or maybe it was simply a case of famous last words. The fact that I cannot remember with precision what her response was, in an otherwise clearly recollected conversation, probably reflects the imprecision of her answer. She could not come up with a coherent rationale for her denunciation of the book. As I reflect in hindsight on that conversation, with the benefit of six months of the Jewish onslaught to guide me, it seems as if the major Jewish agencies issue edicts, as it were. Then the Jewish rank and file simply fall in line. "Theirs not to make reply,/Theirs not to reason why,/ Theirs but to do and die...." The power of the Jewish leadership over their constituency is impressive indeed, the presence of some dissenting voices notwithstanding.

But our conversation was not over yet. It was to take an even more unexpected turn. "Have you heard of the Crown Heights riots?" she enquired, referring to tensions between the Black and Hasidic Jewish communities in Brooklyn, New York. A confrontation had been triggered by the unpunished killing of young Gavin Cato and the maiming of his cousin Angela Cato by a Hasidic vehicle, as the children played on the sidewalk in front of their house. A Jewish student, Yankel Rosenbaum, was killed in the ensuing scuffles. "Yankel Rosenbaum was doing research right here," she said. "He was in here every day, reading the files, just like you. He sat at the same table where we have placed your materials." Even with my own personal Jewish onslaught still many months into the future, this revelation proved a sobering one to me. And as I ponder it with the benefit of a tempestuous hindsight, I wonder what inscrutable fate brought me to this archive, to this conversation, to Yankel Rosenbaum's table, at a time when my authorship of a book called *The Jewish Onslaught* would have seemed a bizarre improbability.

I could not know then that I would ere long be plunged into an intense reading of Jewish and Black-Jewish history, covering many lands and historical periods, as I sought to bring to my situation a more wide-ranging perspective. The onslaught of the last six months now threatens to turn me into an expert on Jewish history. For that I must thank the purveyors of intolerance with whom I have had to do battle of late.

What I offer here is an involved yet detached look at the onslaught against me, from my unique vantage point as both intended victim and historian. This is written in the heat of battle. Perhaps time, further study and more reflection may either modify or enrich the analysis offered here. But the immediacy of analysis can only be captured now.

Over the last six months I have been fairly deluged with articles, books, newspaper clippings, letters, unpublished documents and references for further perusal. As if obeying the orders of an unseen force, well-wishers (known and unknown) have seen to it that my crash course in Black-Jewish history should not be wanting in resource materials. Even the senders of hate and hostile mail have fit into the plan, for their clippings have been useful and informative. I would especially like to thank the following for documentation (mostly unsolicited) which they have generously provided – Dr. Anderson Thompson, Dr. William Strickland, Dr. Michael Williams, Dr. Leonard Jeffries, Dr. Molefi Asante, Elombe Brath, LeGrand H. Clegg, Esq., Steve Cokely, William Jackson-bey, Lisa Davis, the Historical Research Department, *Vibes* magazine, Lenni Brenner, Steve Bloom, Dr. Leo Bertley, Nzinga Ratibisha Heru, Bill Jones, Ernie Stanley and Juanita Harper. I have deliberately left out some names because I feel that their positions may make them particularly vulnerable to pressure. For those that I have inadvertently omitted (and there must be some) my heartfelt thanks.

To my students at Wellesley College who have studied *The Secret Relationship Between Blacks and Jews* for two semesters now, have found nothing wrong with it and have stood fast against the onslaught, my heartfelt thanks.

To my students at Wellesley who have gone on record (in the print media, on radio and on television) in support, my heartfelt thanks. These include (again, at the risk of inadvertently omitting some), Kamilah Yasin, Nalida Lacet, Dahna M. Chandler, Nia Higginbotham, Tanya Jarret, Sara E. Miller, Tanisha R. Landry, Adriane Williams, Caroline Ebanks, Nichole R. Phillips, Thalia V. Shirley, Diane Holmes, Joy Styles, Marisol Rubecindo, Windy Lawrence, April Towner, Cynthia Gibbs, April Thomas, Kristi Jordan, Leslie Serret and Shayna Jordan. To LaTrese Adkins, the great general of the student effort, extra special thanks and praises.

To the student committee who put together a fabulous celebration of my twenty years at Wellesley, in the midst of the onslaught, mere words will not suffice to thank you – thanks anyway to LaTrese Adkins, Tanisha Landry, Azizah Yasin, Susan Epps, Thalia Shirley, Sarra Idris, Kristi Jordan, Debbie Saintil, Faye Holder, Gail Rock, Sara Miller, Diane Holmes, Caroline Ebanks, Mikki Waid, Tracie Key, Tracy Pilgrim, Tanya Samuels, Shayna Jordan, Rhonda Gray and Joy Oakcrum.

To my Wellesley colleague, Terry Tyler, with your brave self, you deserve a medal. Maybe I will commission one.

To Donna Jamison, Deborah Powell Boyd and the other alumnae of my twenty year sojourn at Wellesley who called, wrote, networked and, in some cases, even visited, you are the reason for my twenty years here. Many thanks. To the organizers of the Harlem support rally – Elombe Brath, Robert Harris, Marcus Garvey, Jr. – heartfelt thanks. To the organizers of meetings in other cities – Chicago, Los Angeles, Miami, Washington, DC, Baltimore, Oakland, Toronto, Buffalo, Boston, Brooklyn and elsewhere – heartfelt thanks. To the many sisters who turned up at academic council to show solidarity, thanks and praises. To Jennifer Paull of *Galenstone* for giving me a campus voice when the *Wellesley News* would not, many thanks. To Kellye Nelson of campus radio station WZLY, for also providing me with a campus voice when the *Wellesley News* would not, many thanks. To the *Wellesley News*, which refused to publish my statement in my own behalf, thanks to you too. You were obeying the dictates of a mysterious fate. My statement, published as Broadside No. 1, had a much greater impact than it would have, buried in your stuffy and pretentious pages. From your stupid action to Broadside No. 1 to *The Jewish Onslaught* there runs a line of continuous development.

I now have a substantial file of support letters from around the country and overseas (from as far as Norway), most of them from people I do not know. Disgust at the Jewish onslaught is wide and deep, more so than I myself could have imagined. Several of my correspondents copied their letters to various Wellesley College officials or to the mainstream press (invariably in vain). My gratitude to you is deep.

And to Susan Samantha Epps, chief of many things at The Majority Press, it could not have happened as quickly and efficiently without your help.

Tony Martin
Wellesley, Massachusetts
August 28, 1993

A.

The
Jewish
Onslaught

1

Introduction

In January 1993, I was minding my own business and teaching my Wellesley College survey course on African American History when a funny thing happened. The long arm of Jewish intolerance reached into my classroom. Unknown to me, three student officers of the Jewish Hillel organization (campus B'nai B'rith stablemates of the Anti-Defamation League), sat in on my class and remained for a single period only. Their purpose was to monitor my presentation. As one of them explained in a campus meeting later, Jewish students had noticed *The Secret Relationship Between Blacks and Jews*[1] among my offerings in the school bookstore. The book documents the considerable Jewish involvement in the transatlantic African slave trade, the dissemination of which knowledge they, as Jews, considered an "anti-Semitic" and most "hateful" act.

One hour and ten minutes undercover convinced these three young Jews that I was teaching this book as a legitimate historical work. They seemed to think that it belonged rather in the realm of "hate literature."

There appears to have been some prior collusion between the Hillel students and their adult counterpart, the Anti-Defamation League, for Hillel almost immediately began passing out ADL materials targeting the book. These included, inevitably, an ADL reprint of "Black Demagogues and Pseudo-Scholars" by Harvard University's Henry Louis Gates, Jr.,[2] African America's most notorious Judaeophile. In the weeks and months to come, Gates would be quoted in nearly every attack on my use of the book, as

3

proof that "all" respectable, distinguished and right thinking African American scholars condemned it. The Jews unilaterally anointed Gates with the mantle of head African American scholar in charge of Black academia. He became, in their contrived and wishful thinking, the personification of the entire African American community.

The Hillel activists left my class and headed straight for the president, dean and associate dean of the college. They then went to the current chair of my own department, Africana Studies. Like their elders (for example in the American Israel Public Affairs Committee, by whom Hillel operatives are formally trained in the art of deception and dirty tricks),[3] they evinced a bulldog-like instinct for going after the jugular of their intended victims. For the last three decades of Jewish assaults on Black progress, that jugular has usually meant the economic livelihood of Black people.

By the time that four of the Hillel executive and their rabbi director came to see me they had already mobilized those they perceived of as capable of doing me grievous economic harm. Their task was made considerably less arduous by the fact that the dean of the college, incoming acting president, outgoing chair of the board of trustees, incoming chair of the board of trustees, head and deputy head of the student government, most of the faculty holding endowed chairs and a goodly portion of the tenured faculty, not to mention sundry other persons in high positions, were all Jews. The dean of the college is also on the advisory board of the Friends of Wellesley Hillel.

I invited the Hillel zealots and their rabbi to come to my class where we could have an open discussion. If, as they claimed, it was "anti-Semitic" to let students know that Jews bought, sold and enslaved Africans, then such a generous opportunity to disabuse the minds of my poor deluded students should have been too good to squander. The rabbi thought my offer "a very good idea," but before the appointed day, on more sober reflection, they changed their minds. Bold and fearless in undercover activity, they seemed to have little stomach for honest, open dialogue. Their refusal of my offer did not deter them from later claiming falsely that I refused to meet with them. Elements of the administration, in a frantic effort to find a red herring to "get" me with, seemed for a while to be trying to build a case around this foolishness. They appeared to be trying to construct a case of dereliction of duty on my part for allegedly not meeting with students who wanted to discuss their schoolwork with me, etc.

By the time the Wellesley Hillel set their hostile sights on me, they had amassed considerable experience harassing other Black and Third World people. As relations between Blacks and Jews have deteriorated in recent years, Hillel chapters have become the campus-based shock troops in the ongoing Jewish onslaught against Black progress.

Where local Hillel chapters have lacked the nerve or the inclination to play their appointed role, they have been tongue lashed and otherwise goaded into action by their parents in the adult Jewish organizations and the Jewish media. The visit to Harvard University by Dr. Leonard Jeffries in February 1992 was a case in point. (Dr. Jeffries was at the time under strident Jewish attack for pointing out the Jewish involvement in the African slave trade, among other things. He has since won a court judgment for $400,000.00 against his detractors.)

The Brooklyn *Jewish Press* castigated Jewish Harvard law professor, Alan M. Dershowitz and other Jews for taking "no action...to answer the invitation to Jeffries." The paper itself showed how outside adult Jewish pressure prodded the Harvard Hillel into action. "It is important to note," it said, "that the Hillel Association at Harvard and its director, a Reform Rabbi, Sally Firestone, had decided to do nothing to call attention to the Jeffries appearance....When it became apparent that the Jewish Defense Organization would demonstrate...the Hillel group suddenly became activist and decided to hold a demonstration to avoid the embarrassment of being seen sitting quietly on the sidelines while other Jews bore the brunt of defending Jews on the Harvard campus. As *The Jewish Press* is being published it is expected that Jeffries will speak, but that he will be greeted by a demonstration which will be officially sponsored by the Hillel group at Harvard."[4]

The Hillel group at Wellesley, no doubt responding to this climate of outside adult pressure, had long jumped at any opportunities to hassle whichever Black and Third World personalities happened its way. When in 1991 Professor Edward

Said, a well-known academic commentator on the Palestine situation, spoke on campus, the Hillel group created a hullabaloo. The mixture of lies, half-truths and shrill hyperbole which characterizes the Jewish response to all the events discussed in this book immediately came into play. "Students and faculty have shared their 'outrage at his demagoguery,'" wrote Donna Tarutz, the Hillel director. To this "outrage" she added, for good measure, "'anger at his historical misinterpretation,' and overall disappointment in his expression to the audience." She demanded a "College funded program," possibly organized by Hillel, to "balance" Said's lecture.[5] The co-president of Hillel, speaking "in my capacity as co-president of Wellesley College Hillel, and as a concerned Jewish student on this campus," expressed the trademark Hillel/ADL intolerance for the expression of differing points of view. She voiced her youthful annoyance that "Wellesley chose to associate and represent itself with Edward Said, a spokesman for the Palestinian people...."[6]

When in 1992 African American civil rights leader Rev. Al Sharpton campaigned for the New York Senate at Wellesley College, "Debbie Shapiro, a member of Hillel," made the astonishing allegation that Sharpton was "promoting genocide." "Yes," she was quoted as saying, "He's radical but he advocates murder."[7]

Such immature intolerance did not have far to look for adult example. The doyenne of Wellesley's classicists, the Jewish professor Mary Lefkowitz, Mellon Professor in the Humanities, indulged (with her husband), in imprudent outbursts at college lectures by, among others, Dr. Yosef ben-Jochannon, one of African America's most beloved Egyptologists. At this event especially, question time was thoroughly disrupted by Lefkowitz's outbursts.

These earlier forays by the Wellesley Hillel were watched closely and applauded by the Jewish media. This fact no doubt helped fuel the feeling of overconfidence which characterized Hillel's attack on me in 1993. The *Jewish Press*, "The Largest Independent Anglo-Jewish Weekly Newspaper," according to its masthead, commented extensively on Wellesley Hillel's action against Rev. Sharpton.

The paper focused on "A recent horror story from Wellesley" written by "A young gentile woman from Wellesley" who had joined the Hillel attack on Rev. Sharpton. In the inflammatory slander all too characteristic of Jewish commentary on things African American, the *Jewish Press* recounted "the indignities visited upon her because she opposed an invitation to Al Sharpton to speak at that fashionable campus on the grounds that he was 'an anti-Semite, a hate-monger, and a second rate con-man who exploits the suffering of his people for personal aggrandizement.'"[8]

The "indignities" heaped upon this Gentile woman and her Hillel co-thinkers consisted of a refusal on the part of the African American and Euro-American sponsors of the event to withdraw their invitation to Rev. Sharpton. They correctly refused to be intimidated by the defamatory rantings and ravings of the Hillel crowd and its "young gentile" collaborator.

Meanwhile, heartened by the Jewish media's support of its earlier activities, and buoyed by its access to the highest levels of college administration, Hillel pressed its campaign against me. In the space of a few weeks it would mobilize much larger resources than had been the case in the campaigns against Said, Sharpton and ben-Jochannon. These would include the full weight of the nation's most powerful Jewish "defense" organizations. This time, however, they were confronted by an intended victim who was not a fleeting visitor but a permanent resident on campus, and therefore in a much better position to defend himself.

The campus newspaper, *The Wellesley News*, launched the escalated campaign with a fusillade of lies, distortions and scurrilous attacks that was to continue to the end of the semester.

At the first session of the academic (faculty) council, a Jewish professor and the chair of Africana Studies, Selwyn Cudjoe, made impassioned speeches denouncing me for teaching an "anti-Semitic" text. I responded with a speech of my own during the next faculty meeting a week later. The school's president, Nannerl O. Keohane, who had been absent for the first faculty meeting, began the second with a prepared statement denouncing my use of the book. This was before she had a chance to hear what I had to say. (This affair is now seven months old and the administration has not yet thought of soliciting my views on what has transpired. My twenty years at the college, eighteen of them tenured and fourteen as a full professor, count for little against the fanciful allegations of three Jewish students.)

Denouncing me without a hearing was one of the last things that Keohane did before departing Wellesley for greener pastures, to wit the presidency of Duke University (where Henry Louis Gates, Jr., accompanied by his entourage, had fleetingly sojourned in an endowed chair on his laurel strewn path from Cornell to Harvard).

Mrs. Keohane had probably not finished unpacking her bags at Duke before she was confronted by what must have seemed like a cruel hoax – a straight case of deja vu all over again. Without even waiting for summer to end and fall semester to begin, Black workers at Duke lodged a formal complaint with their new president alleging a Jewish conspiracy against them.

Back at Wellesley, meanwhile, the campus *Wellesley News* refused to publish my statement in my own behalf. They similarly refused to publish a supportive letter from an African American student. I therefore published my statement myself, as Broadside No. 1, "The (No Longer) Secret Relationship Between Blacks and Jews." Broadside No. 1 has been spread around the country and overseas and has been reprinted in its entirety by some African American publications.

Broadside No. 1 seems to have taken Hillel's adult handlers by surprise, for they now abandoned their behind-the-scenes role for a frontal attack. On April 5, 1993 the off-campus Jewish community entered the conflict in great force. In the words of their joint press release, "Four leading Boston-based national and local Jewish organizations, the Anti-Defamation League (ADL), American Jewish Committee (AJC), American Jewish Congress (AJC), and the Jewish Community Relations Council (JCRC) charged today that Professor Anthony Martin, a member of the African American [sic] Studies Department at Wellesley College in Wellesley, Massachusetts has demonstrated clear-cut anti-Semitic prejudice in his classroom and on the Wellesley campus."

The release, on unusually large paper (somewhat akin to a medieval scroll), bore the logos of all four organizations. One of the signatories to the release later said that such a joint Jewish effort against a single individual was without precedent. Responding to a

Jewish caller on a radio talk show, this official explained, apologetically, that the Jewish organizations had agonized over issuing the release in the midst of one of their highest holy celebrations. The matter was of such extreme urgency and importance, however, as to override their religious scruples.

The press release called upon Wellesley College to fire me. Martin Goldman, deputy associate director of the American Jewish Committee, and one of the signatories, explained further in the *Boston Globe* of April 7, 1993, "This is just an attempt to isolate a bigot and let the community know who he is, what he has said and where he is. That is our job." I interpreted this statement as an inflammatory call to the crazy element in the populace to do me harm. Some of the hate mail I have received would appear to support my view.

The release, a cunningly crafted agglomeration of lies and half-truths, was designed, probably with expert legal assistance, to skirt the borders of legality without actually providing easy recourse to a countervailing libel suit. Even so, it may still be legally libelous. It certainly is libelous as that term is understood by the general public.

After the predictable and now hackneyed allegation of "anti-Semitism," the four organizations claimed that I had been the recipient of "sharp criticism" from "colleagues in the African American [sic] Studies Department." In fact the only departmental "colleagues" publicly supporting the Jews is the current chair, Selwyn Cudjoe. Maybe they considered him such an important acquisition that they counted him twice. Similar "sharp criticism" was alleged from "other students (Jewish and non-Jewish) and faculty." In fact, the absence of any significant support for the Jews from the rest of the student and faculty bodies has been a marked feature of the campaign. Neither in the many articles and letters in the student publications, nor in the special meeting of the student senate on the controversy, nor in an all-campus meeting on the issue, nor in academic council, nor in the remarks of non-Jewish students, white and African American, interviewed by newspaper and television reporters, nor in two call-in shows on the campus radio station, was there any significant non-Jewish support for the Jewish charges. The sole exceptions were the president of the college, most of whose top associates were Jewish, Black Cudjoe and Black Marcellus Andrews, an economics professor.

This non-support for the Jews was not lost on Leonard Zakim, executive director of the Anti-Defamation League in New England and a signatory to the press release. He bemoaned the fact, in the Boston *Jewish Advocate*, that my use of *The Secret Relationship* "at a local respected college hardly sparks a whisper, except by Jews."[9]

The Jewish ability to make a lot of "noise" and fill the media with their lies ought not to obscure the narrowness of their support base. The solidarity and support of Black students has been magnificent and many white (and some Asian and Hispanic) students and faculty have proffered written or verbal support.

According to the release, the book "blames Jews for allegedly dominating the slave trade...." Jews did indeed play a major role in the slave trade in Brazil, Curaçao, Suriname, Newport, Rhode Island and elsewhere.

"Professor Martin," the Jewish release continued, "has been challenged in his teaching by numerous professors; Black and white alike." In fact my teaching (as measured by the compulsory and confidential "Student Evaluation Questionnaires"), is consistently among the best in the department. It is often *the* best. If my teaching has been challenged by "numerous professors" then the said professors have spoken very softly, because I have not heard them. The very wording of the charge is incomprehensible and meaningless.

The fact that *The Secret Relationship* was "published...by a non-academically credited source," averred the ADL and its co-religionists, "is reason itself for reviewing Martin's tenure." Whoever drafted this has probably never been inside a university. And I wonder if I would lose my job for assigning one of the "non-academically credited" libelous diatribes the ADL publishes from time to time on "anti-Semitic" Black people.

In what may have been the most unvarnished lie of the entire press release, the ADL and company took precarious refuge behind unspecified "Reports" to accuse me of "unwillingness to allow free and uninhibited questions of the book in class...." It spoke, with similar wanton disregard for the truth, of "numerous complaints of academic misconduct against Professor Martin," which "the Jewish organizations" had "reviewed." In my twenty-seven years of teaching I have never been charged with any such thing, and if I was so "numerously" charged as alleged, I cannot imagine why my accusers would choose the ADL and their co-religionists as the appropriate tribunals of resort. (I would, of course, not dignify the current scurillous campaign of the ADL/Hillel crowd with categorization as a genuine charge of anything.)

"The book has been attacked as being anti-Semitic by leading African-American scholars and historians," said the release as it rolled merrily and mendaciously along. If that is the case, I ask, then how come Henry Louis Gates, Jr. is the only one they seem able to find? And he is not even a historian. (Nor, in his *New York Times* op ed, is there any internal evidence that he read the book.) They further accused the book of using "questionable sources." But almost all of the book's sources are Jewish. Is the ADL in the business of questioning Jewish sources now?

The ADL and cohorts rounded off this litany of lies by sanctimoniously mouthing (from the other side of their collective mouth), "respect" for "the principle of academic freedom...." Perhaps "disrespect" may have been more appropriate and "Defamation League" may be a more accurate appelation for the ADL.

The culminating point of their attack alleged my "refusal to utilize other texts...." There were in fact eight major books and many more supplementary readings assigned for the course in question. But even if this were not the case, the Jewish assertion of a right to choose textbooks for Black professors in Black Studies courses is both laughable and sinister. This type of wished-for censorship would do justice to Nazis, Stalinists and McCarthyites. It has no place here.

For the collectors of trivia, it might be worth noting that this press release marked the appearance of my esteemed chairman, Cudjoe, as a rising star in the Jewish firmament. He was quoted reverentially against me in the closing sections of the document. His services have come at a useful time for the Jewish onslaught and may take some of the pressure off of the overused Henry Louis Gates, Jr. At the time of writing the Jewish organizations have, however, still failed in their effort to find a Black historian to condemn the book. Surely, among the thousands of you all out there, there must be at least one Black historian willing to climb aboard the onslaught bandwaggon. Is there a Black historian in the house?

The Jewish press release intensified the struggle greatly, though in a way that would have been predictable to those familiar with organized Jewry's campaigns against those they would wish to destroy. Every untruth, every deceitful innuendo in the release itself, every dishonest trick in the overall campaign against me, has been replicated against other targets, both Black and non-Black. Former Congressman Paul Findley's book (*They Dare to Speak Out: People and Institutions Confront Israel's Lobby*)[10] proved especially illuminating. I read it after finishing the first draft of *The Jewish Onslaught* and discovered, to my great fascination, that all the dirty Jewish tricks deployed against me fit into a formula that has been fine tuned by repeated application over the years. The press release against me, I now realize, is a classic textbook case study of organized Jewish intimidation.

2

Major Media

Jews have traditionally rejected as "anti-Semitic" all suggestions of their great ownership or control of the major media. Yet here, as in the case of their involvement in the slave trade, one need look no further than their own scholars for documentation. "Jews now hold all seven of the top editorial positions" at the "Jewish-owned" *New York Times*, Charles E. Silberman reported in 1985. He found a similar pattern of Jewish domination in other major newspapers, such as the *Wall Street Journal* and the *Washington Post.* The pattern replicated itself in the television industry, where major newscasters such as Ted Koppel, Mike Wallace, Barbara Walters, Marvin Kalb and others were Jews. "The greatest concentration of Jews" on television he found to be among "the producers who decide which stories will go on the air, and how long, and in what order they will run."[1] If to all this one adds Jewish ownership of the major Hollywood studios, television networks and news magazines, then the picture of Jewish media influence becomes overwhelming.

The very least that can be said in the present case is that Jewish ability to influence the major media is very impressive indeed. The Jewish press release was dated April 5th, 1993 and was presumably received by the local media on or after April 6th. Beginning April 7th, the *Boston Globe* ran four stories in six days, including a Sunday op-ed piece and a full-fledged editorial on "Hate Literature as History." More followed later. All of the first four articles were hostile towards me. Only one solicited my opinions. National Public Radio, the *New York Times* wire service and the Associated Press were among those who spread the story with varying degrees of Jewish bias around the world. (A friend read it in a United States

13

overseas newspaper in Hong Kong. Another saw it on the *Today* show, carried by satellite TV to a hotel room in St. Lucia.) A host of lesser publications followed in the wake of the national media.

The tactic here, as in earlier cases, was to saturate the media with lies and half-truths, make response impossible or difficult, and use this campaign to deprive their target of a job, destroy his reputation, make him as near unemployable as possible, or failing all that, force him to spend the rest of his life apologizing for indiscretions real or imagined.

Lack of any hard information on the situation did not in any way deter the Jews and their supporters in the media from making the most outlandish statements. ABC Television's prime time Sunday morning news program, "The Week With David Brinkley," was arguably the worst offender. The avuncular David Brinkley probably represents for most Americans the personification of veracity and journalistic responsibility. Yet he and his highly respected panel of veteran news analysts provided a pristine but frightening example of the power of the media to defame and misinform.

Panelist Cokie Roberts, who identified herself as a Wellesley alumna asserted, as if it were a matter of general agreement, that I was teaching an "anti-Semitic" book. She then appeared to fabricate from thin air an embellishment to her story which I have not encountered anywhere else, not even among the Hillel fanatics – "And a lot of people say," she alleged, "that the whole course he teaches is wrong in its view of history – false."

Not to be outdone, Brinkley then added his two cents' worth of garbled gobbledegook. With the authoritative air of the blissfully ignorant he piped in – "[Martin] is saying that the Jews were prominent in the slave trade. It was the Portuguese who did that." This would be akin to saying that the members of the Hillel Foundation were not Jews – they were Americans. A large percentage of the early Portuguese slave dealers were in fact Jews. At some times and places in early New World history "Portuguese" and "Jew" were practically synonymous. Portuguese names proliferated, for example, among the early Sephardic Jewish settlers in North America.

Brinkley and company got worse as they moved on. One wanted Wellesley College to fire me because I was not teaching "fact." Another likened my course material to the teaching of 2+2=5. Another opined, "he is tenured and he has a right...to make a perfect ass of himself, which he is doing. That's Wellesley's problem."

"So we don't like what he is teaching," Brinkley suggested at length and at last, in clipped tones of exasperated befuddlement. "What do we do about it?" Cokie, standing no doubt on the privilege of her Wellesley alumna status, proposed a solution – "Let him teach it and let students not take the course and at some point he [sic] becomes a reason not to have him there on the campus, because nobody wants to take his course."[2]

Harvard University's famous Jewish legal luminary, Alan Dershowitz, was quoted in the *Sunday Boston Globe* as calling *The Secret Relationship* "a political-religious-ethnic tract...."[3] This did not sound like the statement of one who had seen the book, let alone read it. Boston's *Jewish Advocate* outdid the major media in publishing "at least ten articles" against the book before ordering a copy. Lawrence Lowenthal, executive director of the American Jewish Committee's Boston outfit, reportedly admitted to a Nation of Islam member that he had not read the book, weeks after denouncing it in print as "one of the most dastardly anti-Semitic acts in American history."[4]

Such distorted access to the major media inevitably raised the question of freedom of speech, though not in the way of Jewish pratings on that subject (as a weapon against those with whom they disagree). For those who can manipulate the commanding heights of the mass media in such ways, free speech is obviously freer than for those with restricted or no access. But preferential access to the mass media was not sufficient for the Jewish organizations. They sought to reinforce their already overwhelming advantage by lies, distortions and restriction of access to those they disagreed with.

The most egregious lie asserted that *The Secret Relationship* attributed to Jews a genetic predisposition to slave trading. This appeared in the *Wellesley News* statement of the Africana Studies department chair. It was widely disseminated by the college administration and made its way into the *Boston Globe* (twice in four days) and ABC Television's *Nightline* program. In the absence of plausible arguments capable of denying substantial Jewish involvement in the slave trade, the Jews preferred to construct and attack an edifice of straw.

The blatant lies had one positive result. They enabled my students to obtain a priceless lesson in the Machiavellian workings of the real world. The *Boston Globe* editorial in particular, with hardly a truthful word in it, came as quite a shock to students who had read the book and had intimately followed the controversy from its inception.

The ultimate Jewish tactic consisted of attempting to silence me altogether. Just as the apprentice bigots at the *Wellesley News* refused to print my rejoinder to their scurrilous attacks, so too their more mature cothinkers at the venerable *Boston Globe* (shortly thereafter bought out by the *New York Times*), refused to publish my letter to the editor, submitted after their four-articles-in-six-days blitz.

While Wellesley's administration saturated the campus, the alumnae community and the press with various statements hostile to me, the dean of the college responded to my attempt to circulate my academic council speech on campus by informing me that I could not use the school's duplicating facilities for such a purpose!

Those major newspapers and TV shows that did allow me a hearing, usually attempted to smother my remarks in the midst of up to six or seven quotes from hostile sources. By some strange coincidence, almost all of the randomly selected typical Wellesley students quoted turned out to be members of the Hillel executive board.

It must be said in all fairness, however, that there were some welcome exceptions to the bias of the major media. A white *Chicago Tribune* reporter spent a day on campus and wrote a thoughtful and balanced article. (He actually read *The Secret Relationship*, unlike many of those who pontificated about it). A couple Boston television talk shows provided fair opportunities for differing points of view. There was at least one major radio talk show whose Jewish host, despite a radically different perspective than mine, was nevertheless professionally courteous and fair.

Dirty Tricks

Jewish lies and distortions were supplemented, perhaps inevitably, by Jewish dirty tricks. The Wellesley College based group, Friends of Wellesley Hillel, among whose board of advisors are to be found the school's dean and several of its faculty members, sent a packet of skewed information to the mother of the Black student who had been most outspoken in my support. A few days later, mysterious fliers appeared on campus linking me to sexual improprieties with the same student.

3

Massa, We Sick?

One of the more successful Jewish tactics has been their ability to find ambitious or alienated Black persons to do their bidding. While not a single Jew on Wellesley's campus has come out openly against the excesses of their coreligionists' campaign, two Black professors have jumped into the fray as standard bearers for the Jews.

One, Africana department chair, Cudjoe, has already been elevated by a grateful ADL to the lofty position of "eminent scholar" (together with Henry Louis Gates, Jr.), in the ADL's latest pamphlet against Black people, which quotes him with deep reverence. Nancy K. Kaufman, executive director of the Jewish Community Relations Council of Greater Boston, has likewise gratefully exalted Cudjoe to the same lofty pinnacle as Gates. She has appointed them both "responsible Black leaders." (In the old days they were called "good negroes"). Kaufman, a signatory to the Jewish press release, was writing in the Boston *Jewish Advocate* of May 14-20, 1993. More Jewish honours will doubtless be heaped upon all concerned.

Wellesley's other Black Jewish spokesman, economics professor Marcellus Andrews, was taken to task by Black students for the most anti-Black statement spawned by the controversy to date. Andrews likened me to a "racist Pied Piper" and wondered "how and why this person [me] has gained a following on campus." He found an answer in the alleged stupidity of Wellesley's Black women. The fact that "(mainly) black students" supported me, he wrote, "confirm[ed] the judgement of many on the faculty that blacks really are intellectually weak and morally lazy." A delighted *Wellesley News* ran this article for two weeks.

19

Malcolm X once observed of the Uncle Tom house negro that when ole massa was ill, Tom would ask, "Massa, *we* sick?" Andrews went one up on poor ole Uncle Tom. In response to the present danger he concluded, "We [he and the Jews?] must" develop "a passion for kicking butt." Whether he had in mind my butt or those of the "intellectually weak and morally lazy" "(mainly) black" women of Wellesley College was not immediately apparent. Nobody has been kicked yet, to the best of my knowledge. I suppose I'll have to watch my back in the fall whenever good ole Marcellus is around. Needless to say, Andrews' article was given much prominence in the packet of information sent out by the Friends of Wellesley Hillel. He himself (or one of his admirers) sent a pre-publication advance typescript copy to one (possibly more) of the Jewish organizations attacking me. When I debated the American Jewish Committee's press release signatory on radio, this gentleman melodramatically and proudly produced and quoted from Andrews' typescript to show that all righteous, good and responsible Negroes at Wellesley were against me, etc. etc. One can confidently expect Professor Andrews to join the ranks of Jewry's "eminent scholars" any day now.

As mentioned previously, Harvard's Afro-American Studies chair, Henry Louis Gates, Jr., has been the (not so) gray eminence of the entire controversy. He was mentioned *ad nauseam* in what began to seem like just about every article, television show, etc. in the major and minor media. In the early days of the imbroglio it was rumoured that he would appear on Wellesley's campus, straighten things out and ride back into the Cambridge sunset. Better counsel may have prevailed, for he was nowhere to be seen.

Instead, several weeks into the controversy, he suddenly appeared in a massive two page spread in the *Boston Globe*. His features, rendered in vivid colour, monopolized the greater portion of one page. For anyone still not dazzled by the large coloured likeness on page one, there was an even larger black and white profiling side view on page two. There was a listing of the multitudinous honours heaped upon him by the grateful powers that be – McArthur Foundation "genius" grant; full professor at age thirty-three; unprecedented full-page op ed in the *New York Times* to denounce *The Secret Relationship Between Blacks and Jews;* a further

New York Times op ed in the midst of the current controversy and for similar purpose; George Polk award for the first *Times* op ed; election into the American Academy of Arts and Sciences; honorary degree from George Washington University; award from the American Publishers Association; fulsome praise from Leonard Zakim, head of the New England Anti-Defamation League; a Rockefeller Foundation grant; a *People* magazine story featuring "Gates and his wife, Sharon, who is white;" 1989 American Book Award; endowed professorships in rapid succession at Cornell, Duke and Harvard; the privilege of bringing his personal faculty entourage with him from Cornell to Duke to Harvard, and much more, too multifaceted to mention.

Surely, the destructive fury unleashed by the Jewish leadership upon those African Americans they disagree with is matched only by the rewards showered upon those who court their favour. The inducements for the Skip Gates wannabes of this world are very real indeed. The *Globe* mega-spread was perhaps correct when it said, with unintended irony, that "Whether by his own smooth calculation or by a combination of circumstances and chutzpah, Gates has become the media darling of African-American academics...."[1]

The more things change, the more they remain the same. Early in the twentieth century, Booker T. Washington, though not an unrelievedly unreconstructed Uncle Tom, nevertheless was not averse to playing the Tom role to achieve his goals. The great anti-lynching organizer Ida B. Wells-Barnett recounted an occasion in Chicago when Washington told a "darkie" joke to a white audience to enhance a fundraising effort. One Mr. Sachs, Jewish representative of the Jewish Julius Rosenwald Fund, liked the joke so much that he retold it the following night to a Black audience seeking philanthropic assistance.

Sachs "laughed very heartily as he told the story," Wells-Barnett recalled, "but when he saw I didn't laugh he asked me if the colored people accepted Mr. Washington as their leader...." Wells-Barnett was very respectful to Washington, but answered Sachs in the following way –

'Rabbi Hirsh is your leading Jew in Chicago....But I am wondering if you Jews would acclaim him so highly if every time he appeared before a gentile audience he would amuse them by telling stories about Jews burning down their stores to get their insurance?' His face turned very red....[2]

The more things change, the more they remain the same. But things finally did change at the eleventh hour in August and September of 1993, as the traditional Civil Rights leadership celebrated the thirtieth anniversary of Martin Luther King, Jr.'s March on Washington. The leadership decided to invite Minister Louis Farrakhan, leader of the Nation of Islam, to address the gathering. Minister Farrakhan is one of African America's most popular and respected leaders. He is also at the top of organized Jewry's African American hate list. For years he has been the butt of every vile epithet that the Jewish spokespeople could conjure up. The scene was therefore set for a showdown of sorts.

The Civil Rights leadership has been struggling for years to ease themselves out of the Tom image. They themselves, like their more radical brethren and sistren, have felt the weight of the Jewish onslaught. When their favourite son, Andrew Young, lost his job as U.S. ambassador to the United Nations in 1979 as a result of Jewish pressure, they momentarily came to their senses. They convened a Black American Leadership Meeting at the NAACP's national office in New York. Out of this came a "Declaration of Independence" from Jewish control of Black organizations.

"Co-convenors of the historic meeting," as they themselves described it, included Rev. Jesse Jackson, Vernon Jordan, then president of the National Urban League, Coretta Scott King, Rev. Joseph Lowery of Martin Luther King's Southern Christian Leadership Conference, Maxine Waters, then a California state assemblywoman (now a member of the United States Congress) and others of similar prominence.

The meeting was indeed historic, for the integrationist leadership finally found a voice that can fairly be described as Black nationalist. They arrived, via their own bitter experience at the hands of the Jews, at the position preached by Marcus Garvey and other nationalist spokespersons for decades. "It was a rare privilege," exulted the event's official document, "to witness the unity and political sophistication of the American Black leadership in New York City on August 22, 1979. According to the NAACP, approximately 200 people representing the leading civil rights organizations, civic groups, churches and some of the most prominent [fraternities] and sororities attended the meeting."

The exultation was almost pathetic. "The bravery in calling such a meeting in spite of expected political fallout," they said, "marks a turning point in the annals of American Black leadership." This was more correctly a turning point for the *integrationist* leadership, since Marcus Garvey, Elijah Muhammad, Malcolm X, Carlos Cooks, Stokely Carmichael (Kwame Ture) and others could long have told them what their own experience now made manifest. "Experience teaches like none other," Shakespeare might have said on this occasion, "but it doth take dreadful high wages." The dreadful high wages of Andrew Young's dismissal now brought the integrationist Civil Rights leadership closer to a Black nationalist position than at any time in its history. "We now have the responsibility," they declared, "of financially supporting the Black national organizations lest we find ourselves under external control and domination."

As the African American constituency which had worked most closely with Jews for the longest time, their new found perspective on Black-Jewish relations was of great historical importance and deserves extensive quotation. Julian Bond read the summit's statement on "Black/Jewish Relations." It was unanimously adopted and said in part –

> ...it is a fact that within the past 20 years some Jewish organizations and intellectuals who were previously identified with the aspirations of Black Americans...became apologists for the racial status quo....Powerful organizations within the Jewish community opposed the interest of the Black community in the *DeFunis*, *Bakke*, and *Weber* cases up to the United States Supreme Court. Beyond that, some Jewish intellectuals gave credence and policy substance to such concepts as "reverse discrimination" and "quotas" as reasons for restricting further attempts to continue to seek remedies for present discrimination against Blacks.
>
> The term "quota" which traditionally meant the *exclusion* of Jews was now being used by Jews to warn against attempts to *include* Blacks....To many Blacks, this seems to be a most perplexing Orwellian perversion of language.

Black America is also deeply concerned with the trade and military alliance that exists between Israel and the illegitimate and oppressive racist regimes in South Africa and Southern Rhodesia.[3]

Jesse Jackson's presidential campaign of 1984, in which Minister Farrakhan played a prominent part, probably brought the integrationist and Black nationalist communities closer together than at any prior time in the twentieth century. Momentum was lost, however, when the Jewish onslaught targeted both Jackson and Farrakhan, dubbing them both "anti-Semitic," painting Farrakhan as an ogre, forcing Jackson to apologize to Jews *ad nauseam* and inducing him to keep Farrakhan at arm's length.

The continuing Jewish onslaught against the entire Black nation, however, and growing consciousness among the Black rank and file, continued to make integrationist-nationalist rapprochement possible. A high point of unity seemed to be reached at the African American-African summit in Gabon, a few months before the 1993 March on Washington. There, the Civil Rights leadership, African leaders and Farrakhan all apparently interacted in a spirit of great cordiality. Back in the United States, the Civil Rights group invited Farrakhan to speak at the March on Washington. The high ground of 1984 appeared to have been regained after nine years of struggle. So the Jewish establishment struck again.

Despite the brave words of their 1979 "Declaration of Independence," the Civil Rights leaders had not achieved total emancipation from Jewish influence. And so one Rabbi David Saperstein of the Religious Action Center of Reform Judaism and "lone representative of a Jewish organization on the executive committee of the Leadership Conference on Civil Rights,"[4] issued an ultimatum. Its recipients were the march organizers, among them Coretta Scott King and Jesse Jackson. "I understand that a tentative decision was made yesterday to invite Rev. Louis Farrakhan," he scolded. "I do not need to tell you what a devastating blow this would be to the solidarity of the coalition supporting the March." He in effect threatened to withdraw the expected support of "hundreds of synagogues and Jewish organizations all over the Eastern seaboard."[5] The Civil Rights establishment capitulated and Farrakhan did not speak.

This time, however, the weight of Black public opinion turned the Jewish victory into a pyrrhic one. Within days the Congressional Black Caucus, augmented by Civil Rights leaders Jesse Jackson, Ben Chavis of the NAACP and others, publicly denounced the decision (though some of them may have participated in it), to exclude Farrakhan from the march. They went further and announced a "covenant" between the Caucus and Farrakhan on legislative matters.

Malcolm X had noted how the 1963 March on Washington was snatched from the grass roots, defused, stage managed and relieved of its sting.[6] Now in 1993 the stratum of leadership that Malcolm called "Uncles" (since the term "Toms," he said, might be libelous), had, after initially faltering, done the right thing. This time the Jewish establishment was left to fulminate ineffectively from a safe distance. "Mainstream black leaders' recent embrace of the Reverend Louis Farrakhan will further strain relations between blacks and Jews," said the Jewish *Forward*, reporting the "warning[s]" of "leaders from both the liberal and conservative wings of the Jewish community...."[7] So for once integrationist and nationalist elements of the African American community found themselves in solidarity against liberal and conservative Jews. *Forward* continued, "Jewish groups say they are watching with alarm as blacks, including the Rev. Jesse Jackson and the heads of the NAACP and the Congressional Black Caucus, make a very public attempt to bring Mr. Farrakhan's Nation of Islam into the mainstream."

With the stand of the Congressional Black Caucus, the Black mainstreamers seem closer than ever to realizing the promise of their 1979 declaration. There, they excoriated the Jews for their "subtle or flagrant threats and coercion or arrogance." They warned that Jews would have to learn to resolve differences with Black folk "by rational discussions and in an atmosphere of mutual respect...." If not, they declared, "realism demands that Blacks will differ with Jews even as Jews will differ with Blacks. Each group will then use whatever power and influence it has to pursue its own goals."[8]

4

Jewish Racism

The youthful editors of *The Wellesley News* showed a mature propensity for bigotry and the major media exhibited an undeniable bias in favour of the Jewish position. Whatever decorous veneer the Jewish onslaught brought to regular news coverage in the major media was, however, more difficult to discern either in the Jewish parochial press or among the Jewish columnists in the major media. It was in the last-mentioned two arenas that Jewish racism was more likely to parade in all its naked ugliness. (All Black folk should read the occasional Jewish newspaper. The result will be a salutary education on Jewish attitudes to African people.) The very lowest expression of Jewish racism was, characteristically, reserved for the clandestine forum of hate mail.

The fundamental, underlying motif of Jewish racism is an unwarranted assumption of Jewish superiority. Jewish commentary on the present controversy has revealed a strong animus against the mere presence of African Americans in the academy. The establishment of Black Studies departments and the hiring of Black faculty have been equated with a lowering of standards. Jews, the recipients of 70 billion dollars in reparations from Germany (as of 1985), routinely argue, and with a straight face, against affirmative action programs to compensate in a minimal way for five hundred years of African American slavery and subjugation. Many have convinced themselves, as one anonymous correspondent informed me, that Jews have "asked for nothing and accomplished what they have through brain power and *hard work*, which makes a lot of others JEALOUS of them [emphasis in original]. Could that," this anonymous Jew enquired of me, "be one of your problems?"

The meanest, most semi-literate Jew (the standard of writing in the Jewish parochial press is often quite abominable), feels at liberty to characterize Black Studies departments as unworthy of academia and their faculty as "ignorant" "charlatans." Any independent Black perspective on Black peoples' history becomes "racist" and "bigoted" if Jews do not agree with it or lack the information to evaluate it. One Jewish alumna writing in the *Wellesley Alumnae Magazine* (Summer 1993) carried this bizarre tendency to a bizarre extreme. For her, "teaching that Jews played a vital role in the slave trade" (which they most assuredly did), was akin to "allow[ing] creationalism to be taught in the biology department or perhaps stop[ping] following rules of grammar in writing classes...." The principal exceptions to the anti-Black-scholars rule are those select few Black academics who do the Jews' bidding. These become "eminent" scholars, however modest their achievements.

A fine example of this type of racism is provided by a regular columnist for the Brooklyn, New York *Jewish Press*, who refers to himself as "Prof." Howard L. Adelson. Like Jewish New York City College professor Michael Levin, who has argued that Blacks are less intelligent than whites,[1] and like pro-Jewish Black Wellesley College professor, Marcellus Andrews (quoted above), who seems to lean in the same direction, Adelson thinks that Blacks are stupid. "Black students," he writes, "and this is a simple statement of fact, for a variety of reasons have not done as well as others under a meritocracy, regardless of the remedial and tutorial work furnished them."[2] What Adelson in fact intimates here is that Black students unfortunate enough to be subjected to inferior pre-college education are irremediable. He contrasts the plight of poor Black students with the privileged (and Jews are the richest religious/ethnic group in the United States). He sees the attempt to help Black students as an assault on the "meritocracy of higher education." While no reasonable person can be against a meritocracy, the term for Adelson and others like him becomes a synonym for the maintenance of privilege based on five hundred years of exploiting Black people.

But Adelson's racist generalizations do not stop at Black students needing remedial help. They embrace the entire population of Blacks in academia, students and professors alike. In what must be the most blanketly bigoted condemnation ever made of an entire academic discipline, he writes –

> The so-called professors who are the denizens of [Black Studies] departments are perhaps the least well prepared of any on the campuses across the country. The poor quality of their scholarship which is, indeed, ludicrous, has made Black Studies programs across this country a source of ridicule in American education. There is not the slightest trace of scientific methodology or technique in the fraudulent productions of the denizens of the Black Studies departments. It would be a pure waste of time to discuss the scholarship emanating from the Black Studies departments....[3]

All of which is Adelson's way of building up to an assault on the humble writer of the present essay. "The current case at Wellesley," he pontificates, "is illustrative of how bad the situation can become." He assigns me, "a rather ignorant professor of Black Studies," to the nethermost reaches of the Black Studies profession, wherein dwell the "unredeemably ignorant" – a fate befitting one who "himself probably owes his appointment to an affirmative action program." And there I languish, in "Prof." Adelson's bigoted fantasies.

"Prof." Adelson's opinions of me and the general Jewish attack on Black Studies have found an important alternative outlet in a developing network of rabidly obscurantist ultra-conservative publications circulating on college campuses around the country. They tend to be run by a new amalgamation of conservative Jews and Gentiles, augmented, in a most fascinating way, by the newest kids on the ultra-conservative block, Asian Indians.

These publications (among them *Heterodoxy*, the Dartmouth College *Review* and the MIT-Wellesley College *Counterpoint*), often rival the parochial Jewish press in anti-Black vitriol, if that can be imagined. Lacking the relative sophistication of the ADL's and

American Jewish Committees, they walk perilously close to the edge of libel and may in fact have crossed the line on occasion.

These publications also represent an alliance of students, faculty and off-campus ultra-conservatives. When "Prof." Adelson's *Jewish Press* galloped to the rescue of Wellesley's "young gentile woman" (quoted above) in her failed bid to prevent Rev. Al Sharpton's appearance on campus, the reference was to a trustee and some time editor-in-chief of the MIT-Wellesley *Counterpoint*. The publication, financed by MIT and Wellesley student association funds and off-campus conservative sources (to wit the Madison Center for Educational Affairs), also enjoys tax exempt status. On its advisory board on a clear day one may see two Jewish recipients of endowed professorships at Wellesley College. One of them, Mary Lefkowitz, Andrew Mellon Professor in the Humanities, has become well known as a national leader of the Jewish onslaught against Afrocentrism in general and me in particular. Not surprisingly, the attack against Black Studies in general and me in particular has received considerable prominence in *Counterpoint's* pages.

Lefkowitz early appeared in the magazine as a humble writer of a letter to the editor. "It has become virtually impossible now," she complained, "to say anything about a minority student or faculty member without having one's personal motives questioned. In this atmosphere," she concluded, "intellectual discourse has become almost impossible...." She was here referring to two of my students, who had responded to her unprovoked and unprincipled attack on my "Africans in Antiquity" course and allied matters, published in the May 6, 1992 *Chronicle of Higher Education*.

Her suggestion in the *Chronicle* that "Afrocentrism poses a threat to the rationalist tradition" may have endeared her to *Counterpoint's* editors. For the latter somehow manage to see in their own publication a "Journal of Rational Discourse and Campus Life." This "rational discourse" sank to a defamatory low in September 1993 when *Counterpoint* (with Lefkowitz now on its advisory board), scurrilously alleged that I received tenure "only after successfully suing the college for racial discrimination...."

As clearly seen in the case of "Prof." Adelson, the columnists of the Jewish community find it difficult to mention the names of Black persons without appending derogatory epithets to them. Lawrence D. Lowenthal, executive director of the New England American Jewish Committee, illustrates this. He became so apoplectic at the legal victory of Dr. Leonard Jeffries against the Jewish-encouraged assault on his freedom of speech, that he momentarily even embraced Arabs and Catholics in his wild rantings. He called Jeffries "Europhobic, anti-Semitic, anti-Arabic and anti-Catholic."[4]

Elsewhere in the Jewish press, Minister Louis Farrakhan is a "professional bigot," Dr. Leonard Jeffries is a "charlatan" and a "virtually criminal" one at that and yours truly is a "career racist." Neither the African American press nor the white Gentile writers of the major media come close to the relentless torrent of hatefully intemperate invective that spews forth in all directions from the Jewish journalists. The Jewish press has carved out for itself an intolerant niche where it will likely remain in splendid isolation for the foreseeable future.

In a time honoured tradition going back many decades, Jewish bigots on occasion resort to humour to make their racist points. The *Boston Jewish Times* of April 29, 1993 carried a full page of cartoon commentary on the Wellesley situation by one "Gribbenes," a Wellesley College alumna. (The copyright notice bore the name "L. Davis.") One vignette represented the image of a young Black woman, "Ms. Washington" (apparently a Jewish nickname for Black people). "Ms. Washington" was reading her acceptance letter from Wellesley College, which read as follows –

> Dear Ms. Washington, We are delighted by your decision to enter Wellesley next fall. Your American Studies course will be taught by Professor David Duke [of Ku Klux Klan fame]; the summer recquired reading list includes the collected works of George Wallace [notorious one time segregationist governor of Alabama], Professor [Wiliam] Shockley [who advocated the sterilizing of African American women to stem the flow of allegedly innately inferior Black babies], and John Birch [after whom the right wing John Birch Society is named].

For a people so openly hateful in public, one can reasonably assume a higher level of intolerance in private. This is amply borne out by the Jewish hate mail I have received since Hillel launched their assault on my class seven months ago. It would probably take a psychoanalyst or psychiatrist to do justice to the deeper meanings embedded in the tortured foolishness that I have received. Perhaps a latter day Frantz Fanon might rise to the occasion.

The beliefs of Professor Michael Levin, "Prof." Adelson and African American Professor Marcellus Andrews in Black inferiority have inevitably found cruder expression in the hate mail. One semi-literate letter bearing a (probably fictitious) name and a West Roxbury, Massachusetts address, but postmarked in Portsmouth, New Hampshire, differentiated "niggers" from "water buffalos" to the detriment of the former. For "niggers" were "subhuman vermon [sic]" while water buffaloes were not.

A strangely similar letter mailed in West Palm Beach, Florida bore a copy of Dr. Leonard Jeffries' photograph adorned with racist graffiti and the following ungrammatical message – "White Jesus and 13 [sic] white apostles as are all whites a superior people. Niggers are the missing link."

Theological disputation proved very popular with the (mostly) anonymous hatemongers. An unknown bigot and bibliophile from Queens, N.Y. kindly sent me several clippings from various sources supplemented by much handwritten exegesis. After accusing me of "Bantu cultural imperialism" he suggested that "The black church is a fraud for the simple reason Christianity is a fraud." This was scribbled on the photocopied title pages of *The Mythmaker: Paul and the Invention of Christianity* by Hyam Maccoby and *The Trial of Jesus of Nazareth* by S.G.F. Brandon. Shifting gears to slavery in the United States, this engaging scribbler wrote – "There was no black Holocaust. Slavery wasn't so bad."

The author of one hate letter tapped (perhaps consciously) into a major historical strain of Jewish racism. He (or she) transcribed the following "biblical" quote for my edification –

Genesis 9:25-27
"Cursed be the nigger Canaan: a slave of slaves shall he be to his brothers for all eternity. God enlarge Japheth and Shem and let Canaan and his issue for all time be their slaves."
So said Jesus.

This is of course the newest rendition of the very old Hamitic Myth, (despite the anachronistic and incongruous inclusion of

Jesus), whereby Noah in the biblical book of Genesis cursed the descendants of his son Ham). The association of Ham with the African race made of this myth a major rationalization for the European enslavement of Africans. For if God himself had ordained that Africans should forever be hewers of wood and drawers of water for the children of Europe and Asia, then the moral dilemma of slavery was resolved. The slavemaster was simply doing God's will.

Christians have customarily borne the brunt of the blame for the Hamitic Myth, and they certainly are not without sin in this regard. Yet, the Hamitic Myth (that is, the association of the African with the supposed curse of Noah), was invented by Jewish talmudic scholars over a thousand years before the transatlantic slave trade began. As important as may have been the Jewish involvement in helping finance and prosecute the Atlantic slave trade (as detailed in *The Secret Relationship Between Blacks and Jews*), their invention of the Hamitic Myth may be of even greater importance, since it provided the moral pretext upon which the entire trade grew and flourished.

Black historians such as J.A. Rogers have long written of the Jewish invention of the Hamitic Myth, but for purposes of this essay it is more appropriate to rely on the testimony of a 1977 Ph.D. dissertation by Harold D. Brackman of California's Jewish Simon Wiesenthal Center. Brackman is author of *Jew on the Brain: A Public Refutation of The Nation of Islam's The Secret Relationship Between Blacks and Jews* (1992). For the year or so after its publication this modest and hastily put together work was the Jewish community's only quasi-academic defense against *The Secret Relationship*. It manifestly failed to stem the tide of the Nation of Islam's book and its weaknesses were elaborately exposed in a three part series by Jewish radical Lenni Brenner in the *New York Amsterdam News*.[5] Which is perhaps why the Anti-Defamation League found it necessary in 1993 to issue an even more modest pamphlet retracing much of the same ground as Brackman's effort while trying to clean up Brackman's more obvious shortcomings.

The importance of Brackman's piece to the Jewish counter-effort became immediately apparent when the Wellesley affair erupted early in 1993. Henry Louis Gates' *New York Times* op ed (in an ADL reprint edition) and Brackman's pamphlet were immediately produced on campus. The Hillel people placed Brackman on library reserve (so that my students could have access to an alternative point of view). Their rabbi adviser sent me a xerox copy and Jewish correspondents to *The Wellesley News* mentioned it often in their letters and articles. Brackman himself entered the fray with a letter to the Africana Studies chair. "Unless I have been misinformed," he wrote, "Tony Martin of your department is having his students read the Nation of Islam's *The Secret Relationship Between Blacks and Jews*....I am taking the liberty of enclosing my critique...in hopes it may aid you in determining whether Wellesley students are being indoctrinated with hate propaganda under the guise of historical scholarship."

Brackman probably considers his own Ph.D. dissertation "hate propaganda" by now. It is replete with information and analysis that most of the Jews attacking me during the last seven months would consider "hateful."[6]

"There is no denying," said Brackman, discussing the Jewish invention of the Hamitic Myth, "that the Babylonian Talmud was the first source to read a Negrophobic content into the episode by stressing Canaan's fraternal connection with Cush." Brackman pointed out further that two third century Jewish "Sages" provided homosexual embellishments for the biblical story as well – "Rab maintained that [Ham] had unmanned Noah, while Samuel claimed that he had buggered him as well."

After emphasizing once again that "talmudic glosses of the [Noah] episode added the stigma of blackness to the fate of enslavement that Noah predicted for Ham's progeny," Brackman turned more particularly to the question of blackness.

The Jewish scholars, he said, advanced two explanations for Ham and his children being turned black. The explanation which follows, and some of the preceding discussion, as already partially seen, have a direct bearing on some of the hate mail I received. Some of the anonymous hatemongers either read Brackman or were very familiar with the historical/religious tradition he described. According to Brackman,

> The more important version of the myth, however, ingeniously ties in the origins of blackness – and of other, real and imagined

Negroid traits – with Noah's Curse itself. According to it, Ham is told by his outraged father that, because you have abused me in the darkness of the night, your children shall be born black and ugly; because you have twisted your head to cause me embarrassment, they shall have kinky hair and red eyes; because your lips jested at my exposure, theirs shall swell; and because you neglected my nakedness, they shall go naked with their shamefully elongated male members exposed for all to see.[7]

Several of the ideas expressed by these Jewish talmudic sages of seventeen hundred years ago recur in the hate mail I received in 1993. The question of swollen lips was expressed this way in a hate letter – "Wet the lips of nigger babies and stick them on a wall out of the way of decent people." The talmudic sage's preoccupation with anal sex (buggery) found this 1993 echo – "Homosexual niggers must use WD-40 instead of vaseline when humping each other since niggers look like African water buffalos." (The references to water buffaloes are doubtless due to the case, well-publicized in 1993, where an Orthodox Jewish student at the University of Pennsylvania, Eden Jacobowitz, used this term to insult African American women students). At least three letters to date (August 1993), contain similar allusions, including explicit references to the Hamitic Myth.

The question of the Hamitic Myth gives to Black-Jewish relations a most bizarre twist. For on the one side you have the Jews, by their own supposition God's chosen people. On the other hand you have the African race, by Jewish invention the recipients of God's implacable curse. This is hardly the basis for a mutually respectful relationship. After years of Jewish hounding, the Roman Catholic Church in 1965 (via its *Nostra Aetate* declaration), withdrew traditional Christian views of Jews as a Christ-killing collectivity. Now it is the turn of the Jews to retract, apologize and pay reparations for their invention of the Hamitic Myth, which killed many millions more than all the anti-Jewish pogroms and holocausts in Europe.

5

Some Jews?

A favourite refrain of those Jews who would even admit of any Jewish involvement in the African holocaust has been the admonition – "You should say 'some Jews.' All Jews were not involved in the slave trade." Nor, I say, were all Christians, or all Arabs. Nor did all Americans invade Grenada. And I am yet to meet the Jewish historian who will tell you that "some Englishmen" established an empire on which the sun never set.

Furthermore, all kinds of Jews, from the Marxist radicals to the redoubtable "Prof." Adelson of the *Jewish Press*, generalize about "the Jews" when it suits them. The "some Jews" business is yet another red herring and attempt at special rules for Jews. It is understood by sensible people everywhere that reasonable generalizations do not necessarily have to include every single last member of a group. If it is acceptable to generalize for everybody else then why, I ask again, are Jews so privileged as to be the sole exception?

If there are "some Jews" at Wellesley College who think that the Hillel people exceeded the bounds of civility in surreptitiously monitoring my class; and that *The Wellesley News* acted wrongly (perhaps even illegally) in denying me (and one black student supporter) access to their pages; and that the administration acted wrongly in sending their one-sided collection of hostile articles to the college community, to the press and to all the school's alumnae, or that they likewise acted wrongly in condemning my use of *The Secret Relationship* without having once discussed the issue with me; or that the Friends of Wellesley Hillel acted contemptibly in sending a hostile package of information to my student's mother; or that the four Jewish organizations were presumptuous and offensive in the extreme in calling on Wellesley College to fire me because they would rather not acknowledge Jewish culpability in the slave trade – if there were "some Jews" at Wellesley whose sense of fair play moved them to identify with any of the above, then they kept their sense of outrage at such palpable wrongdoing strictly to themselves.

The campus ultra-Zionist who is usually in a state of war with the campus Jewish power elite, the power elite themselves, the liberals (like the one who for years has regaled me with stories of her Civil Rights involvement), the former infantile left-wing communist now turned pseudo-liberal Jewish nationalist – all spoke as with one voice on this issue. "It's a lie," they sang in choral unison. "Jews were not an important part of the slave trade. 'Some Jews,' maybe, but that's all. The book is anti-Semitic and you are hateful for using it."

The ex-Civil Rightser was the first to write me a note expressing her disappointment with my choice of reading material. She was also the first to stop talking to me. She has now resumed acknowledging my presence, since I loudly and ostentatiously shouted "hello" in her face in the presence of mutual acquaintances. A high profile liberal actually called and told me off the record that he abhorred the effort to "demonize" me in academic council. When we met, however, it turned out that he was only playing the role of "good cop." He wanted me to remove *The Secret Relationship* from my reading list – because it offended "the Jews."

The only kind Jewish words came from the independent radicals of the New York based Committee to Stop Israel's Arms Traffic with South Africa. Not "some" but practically all Jews who have expressed any opinions on this controversy, seem to have fallen in behind the Hillel/ADL/American Jewish Committee, etc. line.

By contrast, significant elements of the non-Jewish white, Hispanic and Asian communities on campus have been supportive. Support was expressed in varying ways – at academic council, at the student senate, on television, in letters to me and in private conversations.

6

Black Solidarity

The solidarity and support of the African American population has been very gratifying. If out of evil cometh good, then the Jewish onslaught has had its unintended good results. Defense against Jewish extremism has brought together nationalists and socialists, middle and working classes, faculty and students.

And all of this has happened despite a pervasive perception of Jewish power as widespread, overwhelming, ruthless, vindictive and amoral. One of the early writers of a support letter (possibly Black, but race unknown) expressed familiar sentiments when he or she wrote, "What also adds up is these powerful Jewish groups' desire to censor education. They already control Congress through the AIPAC (American Israel Public Affairs Committee), seeing to it that no Congressman survives who votes against Israeli interests." The letter was from "A citizen" and remained otherwise unsigned "because of Jewish terrorist activity in the U.S."

An Irish-American correspondent expressed feelings similar to those expressed by some African Americans verbally when he wrote,

> You are a very brave man. You have to know the power that will be leveled against you....Jewish people in this country have incredible power and don't hesitate to use it to further *their* goals. Nothing stops them – not morality, not truth, not even America's best interests.

Some concerned persons asked me whether my taxes were paid up, for surely "they" would try to get me via the Internal Revenue Service. Others enquired whether my immigration status was tight, for wasn't that the way they got Marcus Garvey? Perhaps most telling for the seriousness with which people viewed Jewish power were the offers of physical protection. Such offers came from one private Black organization, an African American police association and a white (non-Jewish) source.

With the exception of the two Black Wellesley professors who took the Jewish position (and, of course, Henry Louis Gates, Jr.), neither this apprehensiveness at the uses and abuses of Jewish power nor the real rewards of collaboration, were sufficient to hamper the great rush of proferred assistance. The near universality of Black support could be seen in a certain peevishness among Jewish commentators over their inability to subvert it.

On campus Black students remained resolute in the classroom, at academic council (where the administration threatened to invoke a rule limiting student attendance, when they saw the large number of Black students who turned up to hear me speak), through the many visits of television and newspaper reporters to the classroom and campus and despite the Jewish campaign of lies and dirty tricks. When the *Wellesley News* closed its pages to me a Black student gave me access to the campus radio station (and a predominantly white student magazine invited me to use its pages). Even the rumour (no doubt another dirty trick) that students openly supporting me would not receive recommendations proved ineffective in the end, though it did cause some consternation for a while. In the midst of the controversy students celebrated my twentieth anniversary at Wellesley College with a lavish and well-attended ceremony on campus.

Their parents were equally supportive. The mother of a prospective student (who eventually chose another school), introduced herself to me as a former attorney for the NAACP Legal Defense Fund and offered concrete information and advice. The mother of the student who received the offensive materials from the Friends of Wellesley Hillel immediately faxed them to me so that I could be aware of what was going on. Several parents on campus for commencement expressed deep support and understanding. During a speaking engagement in Brooklyn, New York, the mother of a student I had taught at Brown University showed me her son's exam paper from my class (fortunately he had received an A!) and expressed solidarity.

The appearance of the first articles in the *Boston Globe* were a graphic demonstration both of the power of the press (and the Jews' ability to use it) and the depths of Black solidarity. Calls came in from far and near, all offering support. Each new item in the major media (the *New York Times*, the *Chicago Tribune*, the David Brinkley program, etc.), brought new calls. And after the calls came the letters.

The Black press (mostly weeklies), were slower off the mark than either the Jewish press or the major media. A local Black newspaper actually hesitated to scoop the story but covered it after it became a national issue. Once the Black media got going, however, it proved to be a vehicle of great force. Black radio talk shows proved to be on the cutting edge of fearless Black journalism, but some newspapers and at least one Black television program, proved equally independent and fearless.

Support manifested itself very effectively through the network of community organizations of various kinds that crisscross the country. Let no one doubt the power of African American organization or its ability to mobilize quickly and network effectively. A number of rallies was held, from Harlem to Los Angeles, with more to come. Everywhere Broadside No. 1 was reproduced in newspapers and by organizations and individuals. A Harlem rally organized by the Patrice Lumumba Coalition, the African Nationalist Construction Movement and the Universal Negro Improvement Association drew several hundred persons. There a lady offered me a check to start a defense fund. It was with difficulty that I explained that my situation had not yet arrived at that stage. This was a touching moment.

Such wide-ranging solidarity can be explained both by the high level of consciousness currently existing in the African American community and by the widespread feeling that the Jewish onslaught has gone too far.

Consciousness has been facilitated by the Black Books Revolution, now about a decade old. For the first time in our history, Black folk now have the capacity to write, publish, distribute and sell their books without total reliance on white or Jewish establishments at any point along the way. The African American public is reading as never before and they are reading their own authors, writing from their own perspective, as never before. Not too long ago many a Black bookstore, on close examination, would be found to be stocking books on Black subjects overwhelmingly written by non-Africans and more often than not, by Jews. Even now, in 1993, it is still possible to find a large African American Studies department in a large eastern university proposing to establish a Ph.D. program in Black Studies where more than half of the compulsory readings in the bedrock "great Black books" course are by Jews. The reverse situation, of a Judaic Studies Ph.D. program taught by white Jews and based on the writings of Black experts, would be so unthinkable as to be the stuff of comedy. Fortunately, the ludicrous plans of this new Black Studies program, which would have been quite normal in the recent past, are now somewhat anomalous.

The Black Books Revolution is perhaps unique in the avid interest it has stimulated in the non-academic African American community. If anything, the lay population may be reading more of their own material than many of the academics, who have more layers of miseducation to work through before they can emerge into the clear light of self-knowledge.

Frustration at the Black Books Revolution has added fuel to the Jewish onslaught against books such as *The Secret Relationship Between Blacks and Jews*. They cannot prevent its publication, they cannot prevent its distribution and, most frustrating of all, they do not even know who wrote it. The unprecedented full page *New York Times* op ed for Henry Louis Gates, Jr. has done nothing but increase the book's circulation.

An apocryphal Negro of long ago, when ordered by ole massa to put down an African uprising, flung his hands in the air, scratched and shuffled, removed his hat from head to hand, bowed and scraped, shucked and jived, bucked his eyes, looked furtively around (as if dodging unseen ghosts), swallowed hard and finally said, in a plaintive, whimpering, dejected voice, "Boss, I didn't start it and I can't stop it." [With apologies to Malcolm X].

Henry Louis Gates, Jr., spokesman for the Jewish group on the African question, in the midst of his op ed, threw his hands in the air as it were, and admitted sadly, that

> Sober and scholarly looking, [*The Secret Relationship*] may well be one of the most influential books published in the black community in the last 12 months. It is available in black-oriented shops in cities across the nation, even those that specialize in Kente cloth and beads rather than books. It can also be ordered over the phone, by dialing 1-800-48-TRUTH. Meanwhile, the book's conclusions are, in many circles, increasingly treated as damning historical fact.

The African American feeling that Jewish influence has gone too far is fuelled by a long string of assaults since the 1960's, including the Ocean Hill-Brownsville school dispute in Brooklyn, NY in 1968 (where the Jewish community defeated African American efforts at community control of the school system), the Jewish assault on affirmative action (especially as manifested in the Bakke Supreme Court case of 1977), the firing of U.S. ambassador to the United Nations, Andrew Young in 1977 (over his meeting with Palestinians), allegations of police protection of Hasidic Jewish vigilantes in Crown Heights, Brooklyn, the Crown Heights disturbances of 1991 (occasioned by the unpunished vehicular killing of a Black child and the maiming of another by a vehicle in the entourage of the supposed messiah of the Hasidic cult), the successful Jewish assault on the public television documentary "The Liberators" (which highlighted the liberation of Jews in Nazi concentration camps by segregated African American troops in World War II) and much more.

The Black targets of these assaults ran the gamut from poor people to the African American elite. Black resentments therefore ran deep. Henry Louis Gates, Jr., of course, saw things differently. At an Anti-Defamation League conference at Brandeis University in 1992 he "drew perhaps the most dramatic response from the audience," to wit a standing ovation, when he denounced "younger, better educated and wealthier blacks" as "the most bigoted" members of the race and ungrateful for Jewish largesse to boot.[1]

Two of the assaults of this period bore striking resemblance to my own case at Wellesley College. The first involved Dr. E. Fred Dube, a South African born professor at the State University of New York at Stony Brook. Dr. Dube was fired in 1986 despite twice being recommended for tenure by the appropriate university committees. He had given his class twelve possible essay topics, including one on the then highly publicized issue of Zionism as racism. (The General Assembly of the United Nations had recently passed a resolution to that effect).

Using tactics with which I am now very familiar, the Anti-Defamation League and other Jewish organizations and individuals waged a campaign of lies, half-truths and vilification against Dr. Dube. They never approached him directly but went over his head to pressure the school administration, legislators and New York governor, Mario Cuomo. They were able to win the support of the governor and of Clifton Wharton, Jr., Black chancellor of the entire state university system. The result was that Dube lost his job.

The National Conference of Black Lawyers coordinated a "Committee to Support Prof. E. Fred Dube." Using traditional methods that had worked for others before, they launched a national campaign to gather signatures for a newspaper ad and establish support for Dr. Dube's pending lawsuit. Several prominent African Americans lent their signatures to this effort, including Rev. Ben Chavis, now executive head of the NAACP and Hon. Walter E. Fauntroy, member of Congress from Washington, D.C. The campaign was essentially a defensive one, a restrained appeal for fair play which was drowned out by the cacophony of Jewish lies and distortions.

The fact that four prominent Jews had signed the preliminary solicitation of support proved of little consequence to the outcome of this case. The lone liberal or radical Jewish voice crying in the wilderness has more often than not lacked the power to have more than an irritant effect on the major Jewish organizations. Such voices often end up being vilified by the Jewish mainstream as "self-hating Jews." A hate mail writer from Worcester, Massachusetts illustrated this point. He (or she) sent me a sheaf of clippings adorned with much handwritten commentary. One clipping reported a speech by Jonathan Kozol, author of *Savage Inequalities*, on inequities in public education across the United States. My secret correspondent's comment was – "perfect example of another Jew working on your behalf."

In the case of Dr. Leonard Jeffries, chair of Black Studies at City College, New York, the Jewish onslaught finally met the first serious reverse in its twenty-five year rampage. Here was a professor with deep roots in the academic and lay communities, a veteran of many political battles and one with the willingness, ability and popular support to carry the battle to the Jewish juggernaut.

Dr. Jeffries made a speech in August 1991 in which he mentioned, among other things, Jewish involvement in the African slave trade (the same type of information to be found in *The Secret Relationship*). He also referred to the complicity of Jews, as Hollywood moguls, in popularizing the negative stereotypes of Black people disseminated by the film industry.[2] The now familiar campaign of lies, distortions, half-truths and political pressure erupted. The media was, as usual, used to great effect by the Jewish mudslingers, as Jeffries was subjected to a public vilification of stupendous proportions.

In September 1991 a "half-dozen moderate to militant Jewish groups" marched in Manhattan against Jeffries while simultaneously "A militant Jewish group from New York City invaded the leafy suburbs" of his New Jersey home. At the latter affair a scuffle broke out when a Jewish demonstrator called a bystander "nigger."[3]

City College authorities bowed to the pressure and removed Jeffries as chair of Black Studies. Jeffries responded with massive academic and popular support (including support meetings with thousands present and protection from Black police organizations) and a lawsuit. In May 1993 the courts found that Jeffries' first and fourteenth amendment rights (freedom of speech and due process) had been violated and awarded him $400,000.00. Yet the intemperate attacks have continued unabated in the Jewish press and among Jewish columnists in the major media. The lies, vicious name-calling and imputations of wrongdoing on Jeffries' part would appear, to a lay person, to place the Jewish writers in contempt of court.

City College has promised to appeal. The fact remains, however, that this initial Jeffries victory represents a major turning point in the struggle and signals the possibility of further victories, as Black people emerge from the embattled position forced upon them by a quarter century of the Jewish onslaught. The decision in the Jeffries case came just a few months after the outbreak on the Wellesley front, thereby inevitably linking the two.

The Jeffries court victory and the outbreak at Wellesley also coincided with startling revelations concerning ADL and other Jewish spying against African American (and other) organizations and individuals. Beginning in early 1993, the *Los Angeles Times*, the *San Francisco Examiner* and other papers ran a large number of stories on the apparently illegal spying operations of the ADL on the West Coast and across the country. ADL offices were raided and large quantities of documents seized. The two key spies of the initial probe were a San Francisco police inspector (and one time CIA employee) and a paid ADL undercover agent (and one time FBI employee) who had supplied information to the league for approximately forty years. Some 12,000 or more individuals and 950 organizations were said to have been the objects of ADL's unwelcome attention.

Organizations targeted by the ADL ranged from the Ku Klux Klan to Arab-American groups to Mills College, Greenpeace and a variety of Black organizations. Black (and part-Black) targets included the African National Congress (of South Africa), Pan African Congress of Azania, NAACP, the Nation of Islam, African Black Students Organization of San Francisco State University, African National Reparations Organization, American Muslim Mission, Black Consciousness Movement of Azania, Black Studies Department of San Francisco State University, Black United Fund, Mandela Reception Committee, National Conference of Black Lawyers, New Alliance Party, No Justice, No Peace, Patrice Lumumba Coalition, Rainbow Coalition, Republic of New Afrika, Southern Africa Media Center, South West Africa Peoples Organization (SWAPO), *The Black Scholar* magazine, U.S.-Grenada Friendship Society, Women of Color Resource Project, All-African

Peoples Revolutionary Party and others, including several anti-apartheid organizations.

Ethnic associations of all kinds seemed to fascinate the ADL, for they spied on them seemingly indiscriminately, whether Korean, Irish, Filipino, Native American, Palestinian, Chicano, Nicaraguan or anything else. Rival coreligionists did not escape either, as witness the Jewish Defense League and the Simon Wiesenthal Center of Nazi-hunting fame among the files. Pacifica Foundation, and its New York affiliate, WBAI-FM radio, both came under ADL scrutiny. Significantly, both (and sister station KPFK in Los Angeles) are now under intense Jewish pressure for allowing Black programming that the Jews do not approve of. Certain Black programs are threatened with permanent closure and moves have been made in Congress to cut Pacifica's funding.[4] Much of the information gathered on these diverse groups could only have been obtained illegally from law enforcement sources.

The ADL acknowledged, and it was generally known, that they had long supplied information (often with a view to harming those they did not like), to the FBI, police departments, the press, academics, librarians and other entities. What emerged now was a picture of confidential sources within police departments feeding classified information to the ADL, free junkets for police officials to Israel and the ADL itself as a sort of private FBI, keeping tabs on a wide assortment of individuals and groups. Most disturbing were the indications that the ADL and its operatives collaborated with and sold information to the secret services of South Africa and Israel. Despite the fact that this has been a major story on the West Coast for several months, the major Eastern media have been unusually restrained in their coverage, where they have covered it at all. The African American press, particularly the *New York Amsterdam News*, has covered the story extensively.

The Anti-Defamation League's unconvincing attempts to explain away its role in the West Coast scandal raised questions pertinent to the Wellesley and other situations. The ADL constantly asserted its right to keep tabs on "bigots," which would seem to suggest that everybody from the NAACP to the Ku Klux Klan was a bigot. So was someone like myself, a professor discussing the Jewish role in African slavery. As previously mentioned, Martin

Goldman, speaking for the ADL and other Jewish organizations in the wake of their press release against me, said that their purpose was to "isolate a bigot and let the community know who he is, what he has said and where he is. That," he said, "is our job."[5] David A. Lehrer, regional director of the ADL on the West Coast, defended the league's spy operation in very similar terms. The ADL's "mission," he said, is "to expose extremist, racist and anti-Semitic organizations and groups...."[6] This all puts me in the same league as the Ku Klux Klan on one extreme and Greenpeace on the other. A more eclectic and improbable bunch of bigoted bedfellows it would be difficult to imagine. Only the power-crazed and perfervid imaginations of organized Jewry could come up with such intolerant foolishness.

Since there is hardly an African American individual or organization left who has not been labelled anti-Semitic by Jews and their two or three Black surrogates, the logic of the ADL position becomes clear, in all its dangerous paranoia. The entire African American population has now become fair game to have their post office boxes accessed, their Department of Motor Vehicles information divulged and confidential police files shared with the ADL. The fact that the ADL boasts of its influence on legislatures (e.g., re the passage of hate crime legislation modeled on ADL drafts), and on their training of police departments, only compounds the problem. For if the ADL and its fellow Jewish organizations have been, or will be able to communicate to such influential bodies their paranoid and hateful conception of "hate crimes" and bigotry, then the fallout could be grim indeed. In a worst case scenario a Jewish McCarthy might arise who would deprive of a livelihood (or worse) any academic who believes that Jews played an important role in African slavery (which they most assuredly did).

In the wake of the Len Jeffries victory over the Jews, such ominous suggestions have already begun to appear in the Jewish media. One Minoo Southgate of the *Jewish Press*, in an argument defying all the laws of logic, has equated references to Jewish involvement in the slave trade with "fallacious theories" and the espousal of "racist ideas in the classroom." This outlandishly leads her to extract from Jeffries' victory the notion that "a professor [me,

I suppose], teaching Nation of Islam's [sic] unscholarly and racist *Secret Relationship Between Blacks and Jews*" cannot claim protection from the First Amendment (freedom of speech).[7]

A famous Latin quotation asks, "*Quis custodiet custodes?*" ("Who will guard the guards?"). In this case it may be loosely translated as, "Who will spy on the real bigots while they spy on the alleged bigots?"

The language generated by the ADL spying case found another fascinating echo in the rhetoric emanating from Wellesley. The *Heritage Southwest Jewish Press* of Los Angeles reported on March 5, 1993 that ADL officials objected to the "tone" of *Los Angeles Times* reporting of the spy story. This seems to be a standard Jewish fallback position where they cannot controvert the facts proffered against them. The Wellesley College administration put out a similar statement for national and international consumption. They said in effect that they did not care whether *The Secret Relationship* was accurate or not. They did not like its "tone," and that made it anti-Semitic. The book, they said, "is anti-Semitic in both tone and character. We believe this to be true without reference to the accuracy or the inaccuracy of each historical contention contained within its pages."

The uniformity of Jewish rhetoric could also be seen in protestations that the West Coast probe was somehow "targeting" Jews. I was similarly accused of "targeting" Jews for showing that they were involved in the African slave trade.

The Wellesley and Jeffries cases coincided with amazing revelations concerning Joel Spingarn's spying on the NAACP. Spingarn was one of several prominent Jews among the NAACP's white liberal pioneers. For almost thirty years (from 1910), he played major leadership roles in the association serving as both chairman of the board and president. (The NAACP got its first African American president in 1975). During World War I Spingarn was simultaneously a major in the U.S. Army's Military Intelligence Department (MID) and NAACP's chairman of the board. A sixteen month research project by the Memphis *Commercial Appeal* revealed, among other things, that Spingarn "used his [NAACP] post to obtain critical information for MID...."[8]

Marcus Garvey lived up to his reputation as a prophet when, in 1928, he called the white NAACP leadership "spies for the rest of the white race."[9] He earlier said of Spingarn and the others,

> The greatest enemies of the Negro race are among those who hypocritically profess love and fellowship for him, when, in truth, and deep down in their hearts, they despise and hate him. Pseudo-philanthropists and their organizations are killing the Negro. White men and women of the Moorfield Storey, Joel Spingarn, Julius Rosenwald, Oswald Garrison Villard, Congressman Dyer and Mary White Ovington type...are disarming, dis-visioning, dis-ambitioning and fooling the Negro to death. They teach the Negro to look at the whites in a false direction...at the same time distracting the Negro from the real solution and objective of securing nationalism.[10]

Garvey's contemporaries in the Black nationalist community were much clearer on the implications of Jewish leadership of ostensibly Black organizations than the more gullible integrationists of the NAACP. When W.E.B. DuBois, chief Black NAACP spokesman, set out for Liberia in 1924, Garveyite editor John Edward Bruce cabled a West African associate – "DuBois - Crisis - on trip to Africa, bent on mischief....Financed by Joel Spingarn a Jew, and other interests (white) inimical to African independence. Watch him."[11] Bruce anticipated the *Commercial Appeal*'s findings by almost seventy years.

7

Afrocentrism

Afrocentrism is a currently popular term for an idea that is as old as African American scholarly writing. It asserts that African people must interpret their own reality and see the world from their own perspective. Afrocentrism rejects both the claims of racists and the efforts of friendly but paternalistic representatives of other races to speak for the African. "Too long have others spoken for us," said *Freedom's Journal* in the first editorial on the front page of African America's first newspaper, on Friday March 16, 1827 – "We wish to plead our own cause." "The right" to speak for ourselves, said Marcus Garvey in his seminal essay on "African Fundamentalism" in 1924, "is ours and God's. Let contrary sentiment and cross opinions go to the winds." "Too long has the public been deceived by misrepresentations, in things which concern us dearly," continued *Freedom's Journal* in 1827, "though in the estimation of some mere trifles." "Opposition to race independence is the weapon of the enemy to defeat the hopes of an unfortunate people," came Garvey's rejoinder, ringing through the ages one hundred years later. "We are entitled to our own opinions and not obligated to or bound by the opinions of others."[1]

Jews, more than most people, ought to be able to understand these sentiments. Apart from the exceptional occasional work by a Gentile Judaeophile, scholarly writing on the Jewish experience is for all intents and purposes a Jewish monopoly. Even the few African American academic Judaeophiles and converts have refrained (or been prevented) from venturing into the realm of Jewish history, literature and culture. As long as they have attacked fellow Blacks on behalf of Jews they have been lionized most much. In the rare case where they have had the temerity to fleetingly overstep their boundaries, the ever vigilant and intolerant Jewish establishment has jumped on them with the same alacrity usually reserved for those they characterize as "bigots."

Cornel West, Princeton University's director of Afro-American Studies, provides a case in point. He was eagerly pressed into service in Harold Brackman's attack on *The Secret Relationship Between Blacks and Jews*. "The vicious murder of Yankel Rosenbaum in Crown Heights this past summer," wrote West in his afterword to the Brackman pamphlet, "bore chilling testimony to a growing black [sic – lower case] anti-Semitism [sic – upper case] in this country."[2] (The most "chilling" aspect of West's statement was his utter lack of reference to the Hasidic Jewish killing of a Black child, Gavin Cato, and the maiming of another, Angela Cato, together with the police beating of the slain child's father as he tried to extricate his son from beneath a Hasidic vehicle. It was these and other Hasidic and police provocations that led to the disturbances in which the Jew Yankel Rosenbaum was killed. The only thing that West did not do in his afterword was call the events of Crown Heights a "pogrom," as several Jewish writers have done).

Yet, even this amazing example of Black support for the Jewish onslaught could not save West when he stepped out of line. He exceeded the limits of his dispensation when he later tried to move from designated hitter to independent minded critic.

The timing and context of the *New York Times'* publication of West's new musings were more than passing strange. He shared the *Times* op ed page (April 14, 1993), with Henry Louis Gates, Jr. (called into service once again), exactly one week after the first *Boston Globe* article attacking me at the behest of the ADL, American Jewish Committee and other Jewish organizations. Like the huge and seemingly inexplicable public relations spread on Gates in the *Boston Globe*, these articles clearly were part of the grand Jewish design to counter the City College, Wellesley and associated challenges.

In syrupy sweet terms, Gates recalled the halcyon days of the Black-Jewish Civil Rights alliance, a thing of "paradigmatic" import for Jews. He also attacked Black sexists and homophobes, for reasons not quite clear in an article entitled "Black Intellectuals, Jewish Tensions." Gates implied that "genuinely critical dialogue among African Americans" was a rarity and pontificated confidently that "The obligations of black intellectuals are not exhausted by celebration [of blackness, presumably]. Critique, too, can be a form of caring."

West seemed to imagine that Gates' Black "critique" could be applied both to Black folk and to Jews. In his timid article, which was more hostile to Blacks than to Jews, he tiptoed with great trepidation towards the mildest of mild criticisms of Israel. But not before genuflecting to the Jewish onslaught – it was emphatically only "some Jews" who were "against Black progress"; Jews had in the past extended "compassion" to the Black "underdogs"; Black "nationalist spokesmen like Louis Farrakhan and Leonard Jeffries" had "excessively targeted Jewish power"; and, most amazingly, "deals and treaties between Israel and South Africa are not so radically different from those between some black African countries and South Africa." (Massive nuclear and conventional weapons collaboration between Israel and South Africa and the equally massive sanctions-defying diamond traffic between them seemingly ranked equally for West with cordial relations between the likes of Gatsha Buthelezi's KwaZulu bantustan and South Africa. West hewed here so closely to the Jewish establishment line as to be almost indistinguishable from Jewish apologists for the Israel-South Africa link).[3]

But the Jewish establishment would tolerate no criticism from its designated hitters, not even if couched in terms of the most abject self-denigration. A Jewish correspondent to the *Times* accused West of harbouring a "not-so-hidden agenda" for mildly disapproving of Israeli treatment of Palestinians. Two top officials of the American Jewish Committee, likewise pulled out some of their anti-African exaggerations to denounce West's "analogy between former Israeli

Prime Minister Menachem Begin and Yitzhak Shamir and the hatemongers Louis Farrakhan and Leonard Jeffries...."

The timid, apologetic and filiopietistic writings of Gates and West (on the Jewish question) combined with their bold and hostile vitriol on the Black question, are the antithesis of Afrocentrism, with its confident assertion of African equality in the marketplace of ideas. Not surprisingly, therefore, the Jewish onslaught considers Afrocentrism its natural enemy, and has consciously sought to link this idea with the Wellesley and other situations. "Afro-centrist Wellesley professor rejects charges he is anti-Semitic," proclaimed a *Boston Globe* headline, in the second of its four-articles-in-six-days blitz.[4]   "Afrocentrism Is Destroying American Education," proclaimed a *Jewish Press* headline in which "Prof." Adelson praised Gates and Martin Kilson of Harvard and attacked Leonard Jeffries, John Henrik Clarke (the "great paterfamilias of the Afrocentric movement," as Adelson quoted Gates), and Professor Kennell Jackson of Stanford.[5] And long before Mary Lefkowitz became the most widely quoted of my Jewish Wellesley colleagues against my use of *The Secret Relationship*, she had already embarked on a national campaign against my Wellesley College course on "Africans in Antiquity."

The question of the Africanness of ancient Egypt and African influences on early Greek civilization are precisely the areas that have exercised Jews most in their assault on Afrocentrism.

In this campaign the Jewish onslaught has draped itself in the swaddling garments of European civilization and white supremacy. This is a remarkable development, considering the unfortunate experience of Jews at the hands of Europeans. There is hardly a European country which has not expelled Jews at one time or another. From the Romans to the Russians, to the Spaniards and the Germans, it is to Europeans that one must look for the genocide, pogroms, inquisitions and holocausts that punctuate the Jewish historical experience. Yet in the current debate over Afrocentrism it is the Jewish victims of Europe who have emerged as its gratuitous champions and the upholders of Europe's most obscurantist doctrines. Jewish New York City College professor Michael Levin placed himself in the best Nazi tradition with his recent arguments in favour of Black mental inferiority.[6] The American Jewish

Committee's *Commentary* magazine similarly gave Arthur Jensen a forum for similar pronouncements.[7] (Jensen is the most celebrated academic white supremacist of recent years. His ideas on Black inferiority have become orthodoxy for the Jewish onslaught. His arguments were incorporated into the briefs presented by the major Jewish organizations for the Bakke case against affirmative action. His ideas are very apparent in the writings of "Prof." Adelson, discussed earlier).

The reason for this seemingly strange turn of events is as obvious as it is unfortunate. Jews, now the richest group in the United States, with one third of the country's billionaires as of 1992[8] (and less than three per cent of the population), have made a conscious decision to defend their privileged white status in what they might perceive of as the time-honoured way, namely by scapegoating Black folk. "Prof." Adelson, in his usual forthright and engaging fashion, sees it this way – "Ku Klux Klan and white supremacist groups have adopted the vile canard of the black nationalist extremists that *the Jews* [emphasis mine] are not really white or caucasian as a means of ending the full integration that Jews have achieved in the U.S."[9] In other words, "full integration" into white America is predicated on the Caucasianization of Euro-American Jews and, by extension, on the onslaught against African Americans. (Where does this leave the Ethiopian, Yemeni, Indian and other nonwhite Jews who occupy the lower rungs of Israeli society? And where does it leave Black convert Julius Lester? And the ghost of Sammy Davis, Jr.? Also, those who prefer "some Jews" to "the Jews" ought to have a word with "Prof." Adelson).

For the Adelsons of the onslaught it is totally logical to argue in opposition to Afrocentrists, and as Adelson in fact does, that "The ancient Egyptians were obviously white" people "and not black."[10] The whitening of Egypt, like the Hamitic Myth, was a staple in the era of slavery, as a pseudo-scientific rationalization for the enslavement of Africans. So here again the Jewish onslaught places itself more securely into the slavery quagmire from which it seeks to extricate itself.

Arguing that Egypt was white enabled Thomas Jefferson, George William Frederick Hegel[11] and other defenders of slavery to claim that Africans had never been civilized except under the tutelage of the white man, and were therefore good for nothing but hewing wood and drawing water for white people. The whitening of Egypt was therefore nothing but an adjunct of the Hamitic Myth, and by reviving that discredited argument today, Adelson, Lefkowitz and others are simply acknowledging Jewish culpability in the enslavement of Africans.

Marcus Garvey addressed this question in 1923, in response to statements by Drs. Clark Wissler and the famous Frantz Boas, Jewish professor of anthropology at Columbia University. "The white world has always tried to rob and discredit us of our history," Garvey said.

> They tell us that Tut-Ankh-Amen, a King of Egypt, who reigned about the year 1350 B.C. (before Christ), was not a Negro, that the ancient civilization of Egypt and the Pharaohs was not of our race, but that does not make the truth unreal. Every student of history, of impartial mind, knows that the Negro once ruled the world, when white men were savages and barbarians living in caves...that ancient Egypt gave to the world civilization and that Greece and Rome have robbed Egypt of her arts and letters, and taken all the credit to themselves. It is not surprising, however, that white men should resort to every means to keep Negroes in ignorance of their history. It would be a great shock to their pride to admit to the world today that 3,000 years ago black men excelled in government and were the founders and teachers of art, science and literature. The power and sway we once held passed away, but now in the twentieth century we are about to see a return of it in the rebuilding of Africa, yes, a new civilization, a new culture, shall spring up among our people, and the Nile shall once more flow through the land of science, of art, and of literature, wherein will live black men of the highest learning and the highest accomplishments.[12]

The Jewish onslaught has taken its strident insistence on its whiteness, and its "whitenizing" of ancient Egypt, to its logical conclusion. Not content with being the defenders of whiteness and upholders of white supremacy in our time, they have now begun to edge themselves into the role of originators of white Western civilization. "Prof." Adelson as usual is clear on this development. He sees the African American effort to reclaim African history from centuries of European distortions as a "hatred for Western Civilization and the bearers of Western culture. The Afrocentrists," he says, "hate that long line of peoples beginning in the Middle East among the Sumerians (and Egyptians), and continuing in an unbroken line through the Mesopotamians, Jews, Greeks, Romans, and other modern European nations, *who created and developed Western civilization.*"[13] [Emphasis mine]

Boston Herald columnist Don Feder manages to combine a similar idea with a plethora of other Jewish fantasies. "I worry about influential anti-Semites," he writes. "I worry about tenured anti-Semites, like Anthony Martin, senior professor in the Africana Studies Department at nearby Wellesley College and purveyor of...pseudo-historical hate literature...." His "worries" about me lead to worries about Afrocentrism – "Afrocentrism is based on paranoid delusions," he says, with great finality. Which leads him to the presumed Jewish origin of Western civilization – "At the roots of Western civilization stand the Jews....It started at a mountain in the Sinai peninsula 3,300 years ago. The barbarians who would war on the West – Nazis, Marxists, Afrocentrists, multiculturalists – will target the Jews, sooner or later."[14]

The cornerstone of Feder's argument is the fact that "The grandeur of the West is based on monotheism." And Jewish monotheism is what ushers in Western civilization. He neglects the fact that African monotheism predated its Jewish counterpart and that Moses, who imparted monotheism to the Jews, was born and educated in Africa. Jewry's own Sigmund Freud is among the many who have argued that Moses was an African alien who brought a new and foreign doctrine to the Jews.[15]

This Jewish assumption of responsibility for the genesis of western culture can be discerned equally strikingly in the recent writings of Wellesley's Mary Lefkowitz and in her exchanges with Martin Bernal of *Black Athena* fame. Bernal, a Jew, was precipitously and prematurely adopted by many Afrocentrists, for his expose´ of the European de-Africanization of Egypt. Ever anxious to place a white figure at the head of an African movement, *Newsweek* magazine and other major media sources, with much misguided help from Black folk, quickly crowned Bernal white king of the Afrocentrists. Lefkowitz dutifully attacked him as part of her general campaign against Yosef ben-Jochannon, Leonard Jeffries and Afrocentrists in general, myself included.

If any of Bernal's Afrocentric followers had slowed down a bit in their speed reading of *Black Athena*, they would have noticed that he was as much or more concerned with a "Semitic" origin for Greek civilization as for African influence over Greece. This became fascinatingly clear in Lefkowitz's "attacks" on Bernal and in the exchanges that ensued between them. From the first, Lefkowitz was deferential and respectful, in a way very different from her usual anti-Afrocentric outbursts. She also encouraged Bernal's visit to her Wellesley College base. Bernal, for his part, was equally respectful. Despite some polite acknowledgements of difference, Lefkowitz and Bernal actually ended up endorsing white supremacy, making a pitch for possible "Semitic"/Jewish origins of Western civilization and denouncing Afrocentrism. When faced with the Lefkowitz challenge, Bernal preferred to abdicate his potentially precarious Afrocentric throne in favour of "Semitic" solidarity.

Lefkowitz, who appears to have unlimited access to the major media, used the *Wall Street Journal* (of all publications) to make explicit the connection between Afrocentrism, Ancient Egypt and my use of *The Secret Relationship Between Blacks and Jews*. She saw it this way -

> If someone can teach that the Greeks stole their philosophy from Egypt, he might as well claim that Jews (rather than Christian Europeans, Arabs and Africans) were primarily responsible for the 19th century slave trade. At Wellesley, the same instructor [me, of course] who assigns books like the Rev. [sic] G.G.M. James's "Stolen Legacy" in a course on ancient Africa employs the anonymously authored, notoriously anti-Semitic treatise "The Secret Relationship Between Blacks and Jews" in a course on modern U.S. history.[16]

Her contributions to the onslaught, however, actually predated *The Secret Relationship* issue at Wellesley by a full year. The February 10, 1992 issue of the Jewish owned *New Republic* gave her the cover story and eight three-columned, fine-printed pages for a ponderous, rambling and not always coherent scatter-shot barrage against every potential target in sight.

She began by complaining about the student in my "Africans in Antiquity" class who in 1989 wrote an op ed in the campus paper objecting to the portrayal of Cleopatra by white Elizabeth Taylor. With a maturity and sophistication belying her eighteen or nineteen years, the student wrote,

> This critique was sparked by the Wellesley College Greek and Latin departments and Classics Club....Under the boldly written word 'Cleopatra' is a picture of Elizabeth Taylor, suggesting that she resembles Cleopatra....
>
> It was not until the rise of the doctrine of white supremacy that Cleopatra was removed from the black race....In Shakespeare's *Antony and Cleopatra* he describes her as "Tony" and in Act I Scene 5 Cleopatra describes herself as black. However, the strongest testimony to her blackness is her lineage. Cleopatra's father was not a full blooded Greek. Generations after Ptolemy I and many interracial marriages later the Greek ancestry was no longer pure. By the time Cleopatra was born she was almost, if not all, Egyptian....
>
> The theology behind the white Cleopatra is a clear reflection of the racial stereotypes that persist in this country. They believe that Africans and African Americans have made no significant contributions to history and that no prominent civilizations could be anything less than white.[7]

Such confident correctness in one so young was more than Lefkowitz could stand. As the bearer of the self-imposed burden of Western Civilization, she and a colleague actually summoned the student to their office and grilled her for an hour or two in an effort to make her change her mind. Though only in her first year at college, this strong African American woman held her ground against this remarkable display of arrogant intolerance.

Lefkowitz's random fusillade took in Martin Bernal, Socrates' African features, Marcus Garvey (who she tried to turn into an apologist for Black folks' alleged lack of historical heroes), Molefi Asante, Cheikh Anta Diop, George G.M. James, Yosef ben-Jochannon and the Greek historian Herodotus (for writing about African influences on Greek civilization).

For all her verbose rantings, she still never quite dealt with the reality of African influence on Greece. She ignored the work of

William Leo Hansberry[18] and others showing the multitudinous admissions of the Greeks themselves concerning their indebtedness to Egyptians and Ethiopians. The Greeks, unlike their modern alleged descendants, held Africans in great esteem. Their stereotypes for Ethiopians (the most dark-skinned of Africans) were as positive as present day European stereotypes are negative. For Homer and his successors Ethiopians were the tallest and most handsome of people, the most pious, the strongest. The piety of the Ethiopian gods was reflected in the fact that Greek gods journeyed thither annually to sojourn with their Ethiopian counterparts.

Indeed *The Odyssey* of Homer, (together with the *Iliad*, Western civilization's first excursions into writing), begins with Poseidon, Greek god of the sea, away in Ethiopia for a sacrifice of bulls and rams – "and there he was, feasting and enjoying himself mightily...."[19] Homer, with his several references to Ethiopia and Ethiopians, set a precedent for his Greek literary successors who, as Hansberry has shown, referred in their writings more often to Ethiopia than to any other place, except for Greece itself.

Clearly, the ancient Greeks knew more about Africa, were in closer day to day contact with it, held it in greater esteem and felt its influence much more than they did Northern Europe, whose descendants now lay claim to the Greek legacy. Greece was also geographically much closer to Africa than to most of Europe. It is likely that Greece, very familiar with Africa, had never even heard of most of the Northern European communities who now claim her.

Crete, the scene of perhaps the earliest signs of a developing Greek civilization, was even closer to Africa than most of the rest of Greece and was roughly equidistant from Africa and the European mainland. The Minoan civilization of Crete showed signs of African influence (perhaps even involving an African invasion) as early as ca. 3,000 B.C.

The Greek traveller Herodotus, the Europeans' "father of history" (except when he tells the truth about Africa, at which point he becomes the "father of lies"), was expansive in his chronicling of the Greek debt to Africa. Travelling in Egypt in the fifth century BC, he noted the interconnectedness of Egypt and Ethiopia and disagreed with those Greeks and Ionians who argued that Egypt consisted of the Delta area only. Of the 330 pharaohs of Egypt identified for Herodotus by Egyptian priests, 18 were Ethiopian. Sesostris, the only Egyptian king to rule Ethiopia, according to Herodotus, left statues in Ionia, the clothes and weapons of which were half Egyptian and half Ethiopian.

Herodotus attributed to the Egyptians/Ethiopians invention of the twelve month solar calendar, the naming of the twelve gods and pioneering the art of carving in stone. They were the first, he said, to assign altars, images and temples to the gods. They were the first to assign to each day and month a particular deity. They were pioneers of geometry and astrology. They were the most learned nation and possessed more imposing monuments than any other country in the world.

Herodotus specifically noted Greek borrowings, copyings and plagiarisms from Egypt/Ethiopia. He thought that the Greeks learned their calendar from the Egyptians – or at the very least, he said, the Egyptian one was older and better. They took the names of the twelve gods from Egypt. They took the name of Heracles (Hercules) from the Egyptians. They depicted their goddess Io with cow's horns, like the Egyptians did Isis. They took the worship of Dionysus from Egypt.[20] The famous oracles of Ammon (in Libya) and Dodona (in Greece) both had Egyptian origins. Indeed, said Herodotus, "The names of nearly all the gods came to Greece from Egypt."[21] The Egyptians, he said, pioneered ceremonial meetings, liturgies and processions.[22]

Herodotus suggested that Perseus, Greek king of Argos (and Tiryns, according to some accounts), was born in Chemmis, in the Thebes district of Egypt. (According to Greek legends, Perseus married Andromeda, daughter of Cepheus and Cassiopeia, king and queen of Ethiopia. He is said to have also founded the city of Mycenae, made famous by Homer. Their son Perses founded Persia/Iran). Herodotus speculated that the knowledge of geometry must have passed from Egypt to Babylon to Greece.[23]

In her anti-Afrocentric writings Lefkowitz is especially upset at George G.M. James' suggestions (in *Stolen Legacy: The Greeks were Not the Authors of Greek Philosophy, but the People of North Africa, Commonly Called the Egyptians*), that Greeks were guilty of intellectual larceny. She is probably equally upset with Herodotus, who could not have been more explicit in his allegations. In a probable reference to plagiarism by Greek philosopher Pythagoras (among others), Herodotus had this to say –

> The Egyptians say that Demeter and Dionysus are the chief powers in the underworld; and they were also the first people to put forward the doctrine of the immortality of the soul, and to maintain that after death it enters another creature at the moment of that creature's birth....*This theory has been adopted by certain Greek writers, some earlier, some later, who have put it forward as their own.* Their names are known to me, but I refrain from mentioning them.[24] [Emphasis mine.]

Herodotus was equally convinced that Solon, the early Greek philosopher-statesman, adopted some of his ideas from the Pharaoh Amasis, who "established an admirable custom, which Solon borrowed and introduced at Athens where it is still preserved...." The idea was that citizens should annually declare their assets. Inability to account honestly for accumulation of wealth "was punishable by death."[25]

Herodotus suggested also that Homer's *Iliad* was developed around an earlier Egyptian story. Lefkowitz attempted to anachronistically turn Herodotus' account into the supercilious observations of a European on the strange customs of an inferior people. The opposite was in fact true. Herodotus mentioned Greek prostitutes in Naucratis, on the Egyptian Mediterranean coast, and noted that Egyptians would not kiss a Greek or use the same eating utensils as one. All of this runs counter to Lefkowitz's attempt to read twentieth century white supremacist ideas back twenty-five hundred years.

Much of this information was unknown to Lefkowitz, who told me in 1989 that her Greek and Latin department did not teach Book II of Herodotus' *Histories*. (It is mostly in Book II that Herodotus describes his visit to Egypt).

Her lack of familiarity with Herodotus' African trip became painfully apparent when two of my students responded in 1992 to Lefkowitz's *New Republic* article. Relying on superior rank despite her inferior knowledge, she sought to summarily dismiss their arguments. The students, she asserted confidently but wrongly, "seem to have little acquaintance with [Herodotus'] work.

Herodotus does not say that Hercules had Egyptian parents or discuss the doctrine of immortality."[26]

Lefkowitz was embarrassingly and publicly wrong here. We have already quoted Herodotus' reference to the doctrine of immortality. On Heracles/Hercules he said (contrary to Lefkowitz's confident but incorrect assertions), "both the parents of Heracles – Amphitryon and Alcmene – were of Egyptian origin."

Lefkowitz could easily have checked the references provided by my students before rushing headlong into erroneous print. Instead, like "Prof." Adelson of the *Jewish Press*, she preferred to rely on an unfounded assumption of Jewish intellectual superiority over those she considered Afrocentric and therefore academically lightweight.

It is an eloquent testimonial to the power of white Jewish skin privilege that someone so confidently ignorant of basic material in her own discipline should be allowed to proclaim in the *Chronicle of Higher Education* (perhaps the most influential multidisciplinary forum in academia) that "Serious students of the ancient world must rise and protest [at Afrocentric history]. At stake is the integrity not only of our disciplines, but of intellectual inquiry in general." And again, "The Afrocentrists, in my opinion...are destroying what is perhaps the greatest legacy of Greek philosophy – rational thought."[27] One can only assume from such statements by the Lefkowitzes and Adelsons of this world, that to be white and Jewish is *ipso facto* to be rational, however wrong and foolish one might be.

Lefkowitz was equally wrong when, in the *New Republic*, she poured scorn on Herodotus' description of the Egyptians as Black and claimed only one such reference in his *Histories*. There was in fact more than one such reference in Herodotus. "As to the bird being black," he wrote, in discussing the origin of the oracles of Ammon and Dodona, "they merely signify by this that the woman was an Egyptian."[28] On the origin of the Colchians (who live near the Black Sea), he said –

> My own idea on the subject was based first on the fact that they have black skins and wooly hair (not that that amounts to much, as other nations have the same), and secondly, and more especially, on the fact that the Colchians, the Egyptians, and the Ethiopians are the only races which from ancient times have practised

circumcision. The Phoenicians and the Syrians of Palestine themselves admit that they adopted the practise from Egypt....[29]

If Black scholars were to adopt a mindset similar to that of the Lefkowitzes and Adelsons, they could make a stronger case for ancient Greece being a part of the African world, than the case made by their Jewish detractors for whitening Egypt out of Africa.

Lefkowitz's limited knowledge and understanding of the Greek-African connection later became apparent in a debate with Afrocentric scholars over radio station WBAI in New York in Spring 1993. Martin Bernal also pointed out some of her mistakes in the *New Republic*. She nevertheless scored a signal victory when she taunted Bernal into abdicating his precarious Afrocentric throne. Stung by Lefkowitz's assertions in the *New Republic* that "Bernal has helped to provide an apparently respectable underpinning for Afrocentric fantasies,"[30] the white Jewish king of Afrocentricland begged his way back into the dominant group. In language of which Lefkowitz and Adelson would be proud, and which every Black scholar should read, he declared, "I am not an Afrocentrist. I have never been an Afrocentrist. I do not believe that all good things come from any one continent....To conclude, I hate racism of any sort and I am sorry if my work has given encouragement to black racists."[31]

Bernal here, like Lefkowitz, established a dishonest premise (who ever said that "all good things come from" Africa?), and cut his Black admirers loose. As a famous Latin poet once said, *"Timeo Danaos et dona ferentes"* – "Beware of Greeks (or Jews for that matter) bearing gifts" (whether Trojan horses or seemingly liberal books).

Bernal went further and agreed with Lefkowitz (and generations of European exponents of the "Aryan model" which he purports to attack) that the Egyptians were not racially African. He made the astounding statement, which even Lefkowitz may have hesitated to make, that "Lower Egypt was fundamentally North African Caucasoid, but as a consequence of continuing contact with the rest of Africa up the Nile had a much higher proportion of East and Central African physical types than is found in the Maghreb."[32]

This places Bernal in the same league as the "Aryan model" exponents of the past who have seen Egyptians as "dark-skinned Caucasians," Hamites, Semites, swarthy white people and anything but African. It also places him in bed with Jewish white supremacist Professor Michael Levin, who announced on New York radio station WABC that Egyptians were "Caucasoids" and that "All the great achievements of civilization are done by white males."

Nor, protested Bernal to Lefkowitz, did he accept Herodotus' description of Egyptians as Black – "I merely mention Herodotus's reference to the Egyptians as 'black.' I did not write 'negroid' nor did I say that I accepted Herodotus's statement."[33] So for Bernal black is white and negroid is black and negroid is blacker than black. And Lena Horne is Black, but King Tutankhamen (who was much darker than Ms. Horne) was white. Which again brings to mind Marcus Garvey's 1923 question, "Who and what is a Negro?" – and his observation that "The custom of these anthropologists is: whenever a black man...accomplishes anything of importance, he is no longer a Negro."[34]

Garvey may as well have been speaking directly to Bernal when he observed in 1923 –

> Professor George A. Kersnor, head of the Harvard-Boston expedition to the Egyptian Soudan, returned to America early in 1923 and, after describing the genius of the Ethiopians and their high culture during the period of 750 B.C. to 350 A.D. in middle Africa, he declared the Ethiopians were not African Negroes. He described them as dark colored races...showing a mixture of black blood. Imagine a dark colored man in middle Africa being anything else but a Negro. Some white men, whether they be professors or what not, certainly have a wide stretch of imagination.[35]

The most fascinating aspect of the Lefkowitz-Bernal exchange, however, lay in the explicit acknowledgement of Bernal's Jewish agenda. It turns out that, advancing behind a Black smokescreen, he was in fact touting a hypothesis for a Jewish origin of Greek civilization. If Lefkowitz has her way, one will be able to find few Africans in Africa, for all the Jews she places there. She sees the Carthaginians and Phoenicians as somehow Jewish. (One is reminded of the lost tribe of Jews who were once thought by Europeans to have created the Benin bronzes of Nigeria). She also suggests a "Semitic Model" and a "Hebrew Model" of Greek origins. She ended her *New Republic* article, in predictable fashion, evoking obligatory images of the Jewish holocaust. For this purpose she quoted Arnaldo Momigliano, "an Italian Jew, and a refugee...."

Bernal has argued that the title *Black Athena* is somewhat of a misnomer and was chosen by his publishers for its appeal. To Lefkowitz he was most conciliatory on this point – "Although the book has the title *Black Athena*," he apologized, he was also concerned with "what I see as the central role of West Semitic speakers in the formation of Greek civilization."[36] "West" (or East or North or South for that matter) "Semitic" speech does not necessarily transform its users into Jews. But in the ambiguous world of Bernal and the more explicit (though not necessarily informed) world of Lefkowitz, Semitic becomes a synonym for Jew. "It would be helpful," Lefkowitz chided, "if Bernal had explained why the title 'Egyptian' or 'Egypto-Semitic' would not have offered a more precise description of the contents of his study."[37] And she was right. In her exuberance, however, she pulled the clothes off of Emperor Bernal, which was not necessarily in her own best interests.

For Lefkowitz, in dispelling Bernal's carefully crafted Black smokescreen, now hoists them both onto a petard of Bernal's fabrication. (Or, as Black folk might say, she puts them both in a trick bag). For Bernal, in *Black Athena*, placed Count Joseph Arthur de Gobineau, Europe's most celebrated anti-African and anti-Jewish scholar, squarely in bed with the talmudic sages of ancient Jewry, the venerable inventors of the Hamitic Myth. Both de Gobineau and the talmudic scholars classified the Egyptians with the servile descendants of Black Ham. In Bernal's words – "By the middle of the 19th century, Gobineau was reviving the biblical – or to be more precise, the talmudic – scheme, and categorizing the Egyptians as Hamites and virtually black."[39] So Lefkowitz's "Egypto-Semitic" baby comes out Black after a short pregnancy and dies a-borning, hexed by sundry talmudic imprecations of Bernal's revealing.

8

Conclusion

What started as a high-handed action by the students of Wellesley's Hillel, spurred on by their intolerant adult sponsors, has now become an opportunity. The opportunity has already begun to bear fruit. The question of the Jewish role in the African slave trade now engages a wider audience than before. When the rantings and ravings of "anti-Semitism" die down, and the empty ex-cathedra denunciations of the Alan Dershowitzes cease and the peevish prattle of the Lefkowitzes subsides, maybe the Jewish powers-that-be will honestly confront the question – "Were not the Jews an integral part of the African slave trade?" And when the answer comes back in the affirmative, as it must, then the further question will ask itself – "Why, then, deny the undeniable?"

And perhaps somewhere out of all this will come the realization that the frenetic shrieking of organized Jewry that greets any legitimate difference of opinion – the lies, the distortions, the attempts to rob people of their good name and deprive them of a livelihood – will more than likely be counterproductive.

Fear of Jewish power is not as great as it may once have been. Sheer necessity has elicited a growing resistance to the tide of Jewish intolerance threatening to engulf the Black community. Toms are harder to come by and now cost more than before (though it is fair to say that they are by no means an endangered species. Where a pat on the back from ole massa may have sufficed in days of yore, they now want million dollar grants and prestigious appointments. If they are not careful they may price themselves out of the Tom marketplace and bring about their own hoped for

67

demise). In addition, much of the assumed moral righteousness of the Jewish position has been squandered by the excesses of the Anti-Defamation League and the general viciousness of the Jewish onslaught.

A new day of African American confidence may be a-dawning and organized Jewry needs to come to terms with reality. A frank admission of Jewish involvement in the African slave trade may help pave the way for a more mutually dignified relationship between the two groups. Conflict between them is not inevitable, but paternalism and deception have played themselves out. And the sledgehammer assaults of the last twenty-five years increasingly assume the wild and unfocused character of people out of control. This type of reflexive hostility to things Black may create more "anti-Semites" than it cures.

For those of us who teach and write African American history, the Leonard Jeffries case and the publication of *The Secret Relationship Between Blacks and Jews* will prove to be landmark events. For they raise the question, "To what extent can the white group be seen as an undifferentiated mass in its relation to Black people?" Jews constitute perhaps the most distinct sub-group within white North America, with a group life, culture, religion, domestic priorities and international concerns not always on all fours with those of the majority white element. It stands to reason then, that their dealings with Black folk may not always be easily subsumed within the larger white mould.

Seen in this light, Black-white relations assume a new complexity. Much of African American history may eventually have to be rethought and rewritten. For example if, as they now say, most of the whites who participated in the Civil Rights movement were Jews, then maybe the white liberal problem that arose in the 1960's was really a white Jewish problem. And if, as they also say, most of the funding for the mainstream Civil Rights organizations came from Jewish sources, what benefits did Jews derive from this ostensibly Black struggle?

And why did major Zionists like Rabbi Stephen S. Wise and Judge Julian Mack, both some time presidents of the Zionist Organization of America, join the leadership of the assimilationist National Association for the Advancement of Colored People while they, themselves, as Zionists and Jewish nationalists, were simultaneously fighting assimilationism within their own Jewish group? Why, in their opinion, was assimilation bad for Jews and good for "colored people?" Were they really, as Marcus Garvey claimed, spies for the rest of the white race? Or was it because, as white Anglo-Saxon communist Robert Minor suggested, Black nationalism and Pan-Africanism were anti-imperialist while Zionism offered itself as a tool of imperialism?[1]

Israeli prime minister Shimon Peres restated the Zionist-nationalist position against Jewish assimilation in a 1993 Jewish New Year's message, and in terms that Wise and Mack would have endorsed –

> Let me begin by saying that the Jewish people in Israel share the deep concern of our fellow Jews throughout the world, over the demographic future of the Jewish people. The open pluralistic societies as well as other less fortunate ones have given Jews opportunities to integrate; however, they have also posed the greatest challenge to the task of preserving our Jewish identity, the danger of assimilation.[2]

These kinds of ideas are on the face of it much closer to the Black nationalism of Marcus Garvey than to the assimilationism of the early NAACP. Garveyite Carlos Cooks provided an explanation for the apparent paradox of Zionist advocacy of assimilation for Black people. For Zionists, he argued, the spectre of Black economic self-reliance (and hence freedom from economic and other dependency on Jews), seemed a greater danger than consorting in the NAACP with Jewish, white Gentile and African American assimilationists. "Any Black man or group advocating self-determination is the natural enemy of the Jew," said Cooks in 1964.[3] African America's famous journalist and Garveyite, John Edward Bruce, hinted at similar sentiments ca. 1920 or 1921. Bruce came to the defense of Garvey's Universal Negro Improvement Association after its character was impugned by Herbert J. Seligman, the NAACP's Jewish director of publicity. Bruce saw in Seligman's "veiled allusions" proof that "the Jew is as prejudiced to the progress of the Negro as some gentiles who do not wish to see the Negro attain to the standards of independence and full manhood. "[4] For both Cooks and Bruce, forty-six years apart, Jewish hostility to

Black folk seemed to be triggered by African American efforts at independence of thought and action.

Harold Cruse noted the same paradox in the Communist Party of the U.S.A., long a stronghold of Jewish radicals. Even here, in this most assimilationist of organizations, Jews managed to introduce their own nationalist agenda while simultaneously deprecating Black nationalism. Commenting on the 1937 appearance of *Jewish Life*, a party sponsored cultural magazine, Cruse noted that

> while assimilated Jewish-American Communists were leading on the broad fronts in the Communist Party, the unassimilated Communist Jews were upholding the historical purity of Jewish cultural identity in the *same* Communist Party. Of course it goes without saying that the Communist Party assumed that neither the American Negro at large, nor his Negro brethren in the ranks of the Party, had any real cultural identity to defend, especially in cultural publications supported by Party funds.

A similar initiative by Black Communist Party members for, say, a *Black Life* magazine "would have raised the horrible nationalist spectre of a Garveyite inner-party plot." And just as Zionists had no problem influencing the assimilationist NAACP, so too Zionist nationalism found a congenial home within the Communist Party, with the establishment of Israel in 1948. "'Back to Israel' Zionism," commented Cruse, "unlike 'Back to Africa' Garveyism, was neither escapist nor Utopian."[5]

Sociologist Oliver Cromwell Cox explored similar questions in his 1974 article on "Jewish Self-interest in 'Black Pluralism.'" Though himself opposed to Black nationalism, Cox explained an important apparent paradox occurring at the beginning of the current Jewish onslaught in the late 1960's. For the Jews, he argued, attacked Black nationalism while being among its major beneficiaries. Using terminology similar to that of Shimon Peres, he showed that Black nationalists had legitimized the concept of a plural (versus a melting pot) society. This created space for Jews to assert, vigorously and without apprehension, their own nationalistic group interests, without running the risk (as they had done many times throughout history), of appearing to benefit from a host society while maintaining divided loyalties. Cox quoted the 1969 utterances of Albert Vorspan –

> The drive for Black Power is, ideally, opening America to a new and true pluralism in which Jews will be one of the important beneficiary groups....At Cornell University, one-thousand [sic] Jewish students petitioned for special Jewish studies. At Barnard, Jewish students have demanded similar programs. On hundreds of college campuses – and increasingly at the high school level as well – Jews are learning from blacks to confront the roots of their own institutions and to probe their own heritage.[6]

With the legitimization of ethnic pluralism, Jews could now comfortably pursue their independent agenda without provoking charges of anti-Americanness from the Euro-American Gentiles. They could also selectively "integrate" into those aspects of American society that suited their interests. In doing so, however, there would be no feeling of pressure to "integrate" all the way (that is, to assimilate), since other white groups would ostensibly be similarly celebrating their ethnic exclusiveness. It may be that the success of this plan led to a more rapid than envisaged rush to Jewish intermarriage. (Over fifty percent of U.S. Jews who married between 1985 and 1990 did so with partners outside their group).[7] This phenomenon may in turn have triggered Shimon Peres' consternation at the spectre of an invading assimilationism.

Cox showed that Jews (especially through the American Jewish Committee), actually orchestrated a rise in white ethnic consciousness as a means of creating an environment in which their own Jewish separate agenda would not appear threatening. The ethnic movement orchestrated by the AJC "appealed with remarkable success to great research foundations" such as the Ford Foundation, Cox said. It "put out considerable literature (purportedly scientific and impartial) and influenced public information media; and, most spectacularly, it has sponsored an Annual Conference of Ethnic Communities in many large metropolitan centers. In the process of producing these national celebrations," he continued, "the Jewish promoters are largely hidden."[8]

None of this prevented the Adelsons, the Lefkowitzes and organized Jewry from launching their assault on Black folk. As in the time of Marcus Garvey, Jewish nationalism again saw an attack on African American nationalism as a means of thwarting Black ambitions and safeguarding Jewish acceptance into white society. Cox quoted the American Jewish Committee as admitting that "Black-white conflict...was the concern which brought the [Jewish] National Project on Ethnic America into being [in 1968]."[9] "By propagating and legitimizing general white ethnicity," Cox commented, "Jewish unassimibility also may be legitimized."[10]

And what of the labour movement? If Black folk were entrenched in the building trades during and after slavery and were driven out by organized labour, to what extent can one factor in the Jewish leadership of the American Federation of Labour (Samuel Gompers) and the Socialist labour and political movements?

And why did the United States government deny passports to all but a few handpicked African Americans wishing to attend the Paris Peace Conference in 1919, while a high-powered and representative Jewish American delegation attended and participated to great effect? And why was the NAACP's board lukewarm even to its own W.E.B. DuBois' efforts to attend? And why did Judge Julian Mack, Zionist, Jewish nationalist, co-founder of the American Jewish Committee, first president of the American Jewish Congress and NAACP member impose on Marcus Garvey the maximum sentence, the maximum fine and the entire costs of the 1923 trial in a case now universally considered to have been a travesty of justice?[11]

And what of Hollywood, a Jewish "invention," to borrow the terminology of a recent work?[12] What relationship did the Jewish "invention" of Hollywood bear to the unfortunate stereotypes foisted upon an African American people already weighed down under the yoke of lynching, peonage and disfranchisement? To what extent did these stereotypes actually encourage lynching and oppression? And what of other aspects of popular culture? What of the majestic figure of Paul Robeson having to swallow his dignity and sing the "Ol' Man River" lyrics put in his mouth by the Jewish songwriter Oscar Hammerstein, II? –

Niggers all work on de Mississippi
Niggers all work while de white folks play....

Even as I write, the trustees of the North York Board of Education in Toronto have sanctioned a revival of the *Show Boat* production in which these lyrics appear, and over the protests of the local Black population. To add insult to injury they plan to expose schoolchildren to the production, in the name of bringing Black History to the schools. And to the surprise of no one, the ubiquitous Henry Louis Gates, Jr. has turned up as a consultant, in an effort "to placate an angry African community that wants to sink the *Show Boat* they insist is a slave ship."[13]

The questions come pouring out. Black historians must now provide the answers. They have a historic opportunity to open new vistas on African American history. But they must get to work. There is much to be done. Jews cannot absolve themselves from historical enquiry. They do not exist beyond the pale of scholarly scrutiny.

Despite their European travails, indications are that the Jews of North America have, as a group, conformed to the dominant American attitudes toward Black folk. When slavery prevailed in the United States their enthusiasm as slaveholders ensured acceptance by the dominant group. When, in the new world of the twentieth century, liberalism "provided an avenue into public life for those looking beyond the bounds of their ethnic group,"[14] they helped found the NAACP and financed early Civil Rights campaigns. In the latter part of the twentieth century the mood of the ruling class turned to conservatism and Jews, now the country's richest group, again went with the flow. Organized Jewry now finds itself in the vanguard of the conservative backlash against Civil Rights for African Americans. In each era the Jewish attitude to Black people has provided the credentials for their membership in the mainstream.

But whatever the period – slave, liberal or conservative, the constant has been a Jewish insistence on the right to monitor the activities of African Americans. Slavery was the ultimate monitoring device. Without freedom of movement, expression or anything else, and subject to a perpetual curfew, the slave spent his whole life under the fixed scrutiny of the slavemaster. In the age of liberalism, scrutiny was exercised by those who founded, led and funded the assimilationist Black organizations. From Joel Spingarn using his perch as president of the NAACP to spy for military intelligence, to Stanley Levison drafting Martin Luther King, Jr.'s speeches, the incessant liberal monitoring of Black activity was no less oppressive, if even more sophisticated, than during the era of slavery. The supposedly radical Communist Party was no different from the liberals, with a Jew firmly ensconced as head of the Harlem branch up to the late 1930's.[15] And now in the era of conservatism, we discover that the Anti-Defamation League is spying on everything Black, from the NAACP to the African National Congress of South Africa.

It was coincidentally the African National Congress which unwittingly provided the occasion for one of the Jewish establishment's more overt attempts to dictate to Black people. In the process there appeared on the record as clear a statement of Jewry's conception of its power in the United States political system as one is likely to find.

On June 21, 1990 the ABC Television program *Nightline* aired a special New York town meeting with the ANC's Nelson Mandela, recently released from twenty seven years in prison, and on a triumphant tour of the United States. Israel's nuclear collaboration with South Africa and its sanctions-defying diamond and weapons trade with the white supremacist apartheid state were by then well known. So was the fact that South Africa's Jews, beneficiaries of apartheid, were the world's richest community and the world's highest per capita contributors to Israel.[16]

Still, under the direction of the program's Jewish moderator, Ted Koppel, the town meeting quickly developed into one more battleground of the Jewish onslaught. One Ken Adelman of the Institute for Contemporary Studies, Henry Siegman, executive director of the American Jewish Congress and Koppel, as if by prearrangement, all sought to dictate to Mandela what the ANC's position should be on Yasir Arafat and the Palestinian struggle.

Drawn out by the wily Mandela, Koppel abandoned his euphemism-laden innuendoes and stated frankly that he saw this as a Black-Jewish problem. "There has been for many years a close alliance between the Jewish population and the Black population in the Civil Rights struggle," Koppel alleged. "There is likely to be a rather negative reaction" to the ANC's refusal to renounce comradely ties with Arafat, Koppel threatened. "That reaction," he continued, "could very well cause [Jewish] people to call up their congressmen, their senators" and urge action against the ANC's request for a continuation of sanctions against the apartheid regime.

Mandela's response to the three pronged attack was to lecture his inquisitors in his headmasterly way – "One of the mistakes which some political analysts make is to think that their enemies should be our enemies." The Black section of the audience cheered lustily while Jesse Jackson and New York Mayor, David Dinkins, both victims of the Jewish onslaught, huddled together poker faced and inscrutable in the front seat. But not before Koppel, perhaps in an unguarded moment, impressed Mandela and the world with the awesomeness of Jewish power in these United States. Mandela, Koppel warned, should "have been more concerned about not alienating" American Jews, *who have it within their hands, within their power* [emphasis mine] either to continue sanctions against South Africa or to raise those sanctions, to lift them."

Perhaps the most insidious manifestation of this assumption of overseership is to be found in the Jewish penchant for opinion polls. Some Jewish organization or other is forever polling Black folk or polling white people about Black folk. The World Jewish Congress and World Zionist Organization were bold enough in 1984 to send a Jewish woman, one Kitty Cohen, to poll the Congressional Black Caucus. (And sixteen of the Caucus' twenty-one members were injudicious enough to cooperate).[17] Even in 1993, with its spy operation exposed and a libelous document on the market branding every Black person it can think of as anti-Semitic, the ADL can still induce the major media to report its latest "findings" on white racism against Black folk.

The monitoring impulse is also developed to a high degree in academia. For most of the twentieth century, as already mentioned, Jews have been a major factor in Black Studies scholarship. Every other Jew you meet in the social sciences and humanities today claims some expertise in the study of Black people. This would be fine if most of these scholars had some genuine love for the African (as a few perhaps do), and if Africans were equally clambering all over Jewish Studies. Yet one would not require prophetic insight to foretell that any African American scholar brave enough to claim expertise in Judaic Studies would more than likely be met with the usual howls of "anti-Semitism" – unless, perhaps, such a scholar were uncritically praiseworthy of everything Jews have ever done, from biblical times to the present.

On a recent radio debate on the Jewish question with the deputy executive director of the American Jewish Committee in Boston, I discovered that both my opponent and the talkshow host (a Jew), were Ph.D.'s who had taught Black History at college level. Yet they both held the most obscurantist views on Black folk. They were also both surprisingly ignorant of some aspects of their own history, leading me to surmise that there must be more academic Jews monitoring Black folk than studying themselves.

The insufferable presumptuousness of this historical tendency finds its ultimate expression when three young Hillel student operatives can confidently assume that they have a right to clandestinely sit in on my class to monitor proceedings. If their elders are any indication they probably did not even know that there were Jews in the United States before 1880. They probably never heard of Sephardic Aaron Lopez, slaveship owner extraordinaire of Newport, or the slave dealing Dutch West India Company, with its Jewish investors, or Jew Savannah in Suriname, with its indescribably cruel slaveowners. Yet, young and foolish as they were, they nevertheless felt empowered, by a combination of white skin privilege and a five hundred year legacy of Jewish overseership of Black people, to persist in their foolishness. And the fact that the college administration and the national media took them seriously only shows that power needs neither to be right nor responsible. "I am disturbed stronger action has not been taken [against Tony Martin]," wailed Hillel monitor Laura Kossoff in the *Boston Jewish Times*. Kossoff was sometime vice-president of the Wellesley Hillel. "He's got free reign," whined Adena Katz, chief spokesperson for the monitoring posse, "and he's going to do it [teach *The Secret Relationship*] forever until someone stops him."[18] "There is no justice but strength," said Marcus Garvey. Black people must get strong, lest the most foolish among the presently strong continue to harbour delusions of authority over their elders and betters of sable hue.

Black folk will continue to be the pawns in other people's games until the elusive quest for power is realized. It may be that the Jewish establishment has concluded that a prostrate African American population, to be oppressed or paternalized as the times warrant, will continue to be its insurance against a Euro-American reversion to European anti-Jewish activity.

This would partly explain the historical hostility to Black organizations preaching self-reliance (Marcus Garvey's Universal Negro Improvement Association, the Nation of Islam, the Black Power movement, etc). It would also help explain the frenzied attacks on Afrocentrism and the strident efforts to associate Jews with whiteness and the origins of Western civilization. For a self-reliant, independently thinking, politically and economically powerful African American entity would deprive the Jewish leadership of the perceived basis for the maintenance of their comfort level within the Euro-American structure.

For Black people to remain the perpetual pawns in someone else's game would of course be intolerable and a fulfillment of the Hamitic Myth. Jews must find some other way to maintain their comfort level in European America. They could indeed bring much to a mutually beneficial relationship with African Americans, though not in the illusory "Civil Rights alliance" mould of *ex post facto* invention. Nor can a simplistic application of the "equal suffering" argument take us very far. Fresh memories of the Roman destruction of Jerusalem did not prevent the Talmudic scholars from inventing the Hamitic Myth. Fresh memories of the inquisition did not prevent Sephardic Jews from becoming major participants in the slave trade. And fresh memories of the Jewish holocaust certainly have not blunted the present onslaught.

Any meaningful relationship will naturally have to begin with dialogue. And the Black designated hitters of the Jewish onslaught will be of little use in such conversations, except maybe as officially acknowledged paid agents for an extraneous entity.

Jews might also profitably emulate the Roman Catholic Church, which has apologized to Jews, Native Americans and Africans for past indiscretions. Pope John Paul II used the quincentennial of Columbus' New World explorations to apologize for the church's role in the enslavement and extermination of Africans and Native Americans.[19]

The Jews will also derive much moral profit from an emulation of the Germans, who had already paid them 70 billion dollars worth of reparations as of 1985.

Dialogue. Apologies. Reparations.

Notes

1. Introduction

1. Published by the Historical Research Department, Nation of Islam, Boston, MA, 1991.
2. *New York Times,* July 20, 1992.
3. Paul Findley, *They Dare to Speak Out: People and Institutions Confront Israel's Lobby* (Westport, CT: Lawrence Hill and Co., 1985), pp. 180ff.
4. February 7 to 13, 1992.
5. *Wellesley News,* October 23, 1991.
6. Ibid.
7. Ibid, March 18, 1992.
8. *Jewish Press,* April 9, 1993.
9. Boston *Jewish Advocate,* March 6-11, 1993.
10. (Westport, CT: Lawrence Hill and Co., 1985), especially the chapters on "Challenges to Academic Freedom" and "Tucson: Case Study in Intimidation."

2. Major Media

1. Charles E. Silberman, *A Certain People: American Jews and Their Lives Today* (New York: Summit Books, 1985), pp. 152-155.
2. Quotations transcribed from David Brinkley's program by the author.
3. April 11, 1993.
4. *Blacks and Jews News,* Spring 1993, p. 2.

3. Massa, We Sick?

1. *Boston Globe,* April 29, 1993.
2. Alfreda M. Duster, Ed., *Crusade for Justice: The Autobiography of Ida B. Wells* (Chicago: University of Chicago Press, 1970), p. 331.
3. Ben Johnson, Ed., *A Declaration of Independence: Black American Leadership Summit, New York, NY, August 22, 1979* (Ben Johnson: Washington, D.C., 1979), pp. 2, 7 et passim.
4. *Forward,* October 1, 1993.

5. The text of Saperstein's "Confidential and Personal" letter is in *The Final Call*, September 22, 1993.
6. *Malcolm X Speaks* (George Breitman, Ed.), (New York: Grove Press, 1965), pp. 14-15.
7. *Forward*, September 24, 1993.
8. *A Declaration of Independence*, p. 8.

4. Jewish Racism

1. *New York Times*, April 20, 1990.
2. *Jewish Press*, June 11, 1993.
3. Ibid, May 14, 1993.
4. Boston *Jewish Advocate*, June 11-17, 1993.
5. September 26, October 3 and 10, 1992.
6. See Harold D. Brackman, "The Ebb and Flow of Conflict: A History of Black-Jewish Relations through 1900," Ph.D. dissertation, UCLA, 1977.
7. Ibid, pp. 80, 81.

6. Black Solidarity

1. *Boston Globe*, November 7, 1992.
2. For the text of the speech see Leonard Jeffries, *Our Sacred Mission* (Los Angeles: ASCAC Foundation, 1991).
3. *New York Times*, September 16, 1991.
4. *New York Amsterdam News*, August 21, 1993.
5. *Boston Globe*, April 7, 1993.
6. *Los Angeles Times*, February 28, 1993.
7. *Jewish Press*, August 13, 1993.
8. *Commercial Appeal*, March 21, 1993.
9. *Negro World* (New York), October 6, 1928, quoted in Tony Martin, *Race First: the Ideological and Organizational Struggles of Marcus Garvey and the Universal Negro Improvement Association* (Dover, MA: The Majority Press, 1986, first pub. 1976), p. 274.
10. Amy Jacques Garvey, Ed., *The Philosophy and Opinions of Marcus Garvey* (Dover, MA: The Majority Press, reprint of 1923 and 1925 editions), II, p. 70.
11. Bruce to Florence (his wife), January 2, 1924, John E. Bruce Papers, MsL33, Schomburg Center, New York Public Library, quoted in Martin, *Race First*, op. cit., p. 136.

7. Afrocentrism

1. In Tony Martin, Comp., *African Fundamentalism: A Literary and Cultural Anthology of Garvey's Harlem Renaissance* (Dover, MA: The Majority Press, 1991), p. 4.

2. Cornel West, "Afterword," in Harold Brackman, *Jew on the Brain* (1992), p. 67.

3. San Francisco *Jewish Bulletin*, August 30, 1985, quoted in Lenni Brenner, *Jews in America Today* (Secaucus, NJ: Lyle Stuart, 1986), p. 257.

4. April 9, 1993.

5. August 14, 1992.

6. *New York Times*, April 20, 1990.

7. Joel Dreyfuss and Charles Lawrence III, *The Bakke Case: The Politics of Inequality* (New York: Harcourt Brace Jovanovich, 1979), p. 155.

8. Lenni Brenner and Steve Bloom, *The Crisis in Black-Jewish Relations* (New York: Committee to Stop Israel's Arms Traffic with South Africa, 1993), p. 3, quoting *Forbes* magazine, October 19, 1992.

9. *Jewish Press*, August 21, 1992.

10. Ibid, August 14, 1992.

11. See Thomas Jefferson, *Notes on the State of Virginia* (New York: Norton, 1972 edition) and George W. F. Hegel, *The Philosophy of History* (London: Colonial Press, ca. 1900).

12. Amy Jacques Garvey, Ed., *The Philosophy and Opinions of Marcus Garvey* (Dover, MA: The Majority Press, reprint of 1923 and 1925 editions), II, p. 19.

13. *Jewish Press*, August 14, 1992.

14. *Boston Herald*, April 29, 1993.

15. Sigmund Freud, *Moses and Monotheism* (New York: Vintage Books, 1939).

16. *Wall Street Journal*, April 7, 1993.

17. Anana Evans, "The Myth and Reality of Cleopatra," *Wellesley News*, October 25, 1989.

18. Joseph E. Harris, *Africa and Africans as Seen by Classical Writers. The William Leo Hansberry African History Notebook, Vol. II* (Washington, DC: Howard University Press, 1977).

19. Homer, *Odyssey*, trans. by W.H.D. Rouse (New York: New American Library, 1937), p. 11.

20. Herodotus, *The Histories* (London: Penguin, 1954), trans. by Aubrey de Sélincourt, revised by A.R. Burn, p. 149.

21. Ibid, p. 149.

22. Ibid, p. 152.

23. Ibid, p. 169.

24. Ibid, p. 178.

25. Ibid, p. 199.
26. *Wellesley News*, May 5, 1992.
27. Herodotus, *Histories*, p. 146.
28. *Chronicle of Higher Education*, May 6, 1992.
29. Herodotus, *Histories*, p. 152.
30. Ibid, p. 167.
31. *New Republic*, February 10, 1992.
32. Ibid, March 9, 1992.
33. Ibid.
34. Ibid.
35. Garvey, *Philosophy and Opinions*, op. cit., II, p. 18.
36. Ibid, p. 19.
37. *New Republic*, March 9, 1992.
38. Ibid.
39. Martin Bernal, *Black Athena: the Afroasiatic Roots of Classical Civilization*, I, *The Fabrication of Ancient Greece, 1785-1985* (New Brunswick, NJ: Rutgers University Press, 1987), p. 245.

8. Conclusion

1. *Daily Worker*, August 18, 1924, quoted in Tony Martin, *Race First: the Ideological and Organizational Struggles of Marcus Garvey and the UNIA* (Dover, MA: The Majority Press, 1986, first pub. 1976), pp. 243-44.
2. *New York Amsterdam News*, September 11, 1993.
3. Robert Harris et al, *Carlos Cooks: And Black Nationalism from Garvey to Malcolm* (Dover, MA: The Majority Press, 1992), p.125.
4. John E. Bruce Papers, Group D-9E, 40-9, Schomburg Center, New York Public Library.
5. Harold Cruse, *The Crisis of the Negro Intellectual* (New York: William Morrow and Co., 1967), pp. 148, 149, 164, 164n. For the Communist Party's campaign against Garvey's nationalism see Tony Martin, *Race First: the Ideological and Organizational Struggles of Marcus Garvey and the Universal Negro Improvement Association* (Dover, MA: The Majority Press, 1986, first pub. 1976), pp. 221-272.
6. Oliver C. Cox, "Jewish Self-interest in 'Black Pluralism,'" *The Sociological Quarterly* 15 (Spring 1974), p. 188, quoting Albert Vorspan, "Blacks and Jews," in Nat Hentoff, Ed., *Black Anti-Semitism and Jewish Racism* (New York: Richard W. Baron Pub. Co., 1969), p. 220.
7. Lenni Brenner and Steve Bloom, *The Crisis in Black-Jewish Relations* (New York: CSIATSA, 1993), p. 9.
8. Cox, "Jewish Self-interest," op. cit., p. 192.
9. Ibid, p. 191, quoting American Jewish Commitee, "The Group Life Report," No. 2, January 1972, mimeographed document.

10. Cox, op. cit., p. 191.
11. Several Garvey scholars, the present author included, testified to this effect at a Congressional hearing in July 1987 – United States House of Representatives, House Judiciary Committee, Sub-committee on Criminal Justice, hearings on a bill to exonerate Marcus Garvey, July 28, 1987. The bill was introduced by Congressman Charles Rangel (Democrat - New York).
12. Neal Gabler, *An Empire of Their Own: How the Jews Invented Hollywood* (New York: Anchor Books, 1988).
13. *Vibes International* (Detroit), III, 10, 1993, p. 20. Norman Richmond, "The Hidden History of Black Resistance," *Toronto Star*, June 15, 1993.
14. Arthur A. Goren, *The American Jews* (Cambridge, Mass.: The Belknap Press at Harvard University Press, 1982), p. 98.
15. Cruse, *Crisis of the Negro Intellectual*, p. 163.
16. Steven E. Aschheim, "The Communal Organization of South African Jewry," *The Jewish Journal of Sociology*, XII, 2, p. 214.
17. Lenni Brenner, *Jews in America Today* (Secaucus, NJ: Lyle Stuart, 1986), p. 249.
18. *Boston Jewish Times*, April 15, 1993.
19. *Boston Globe*, August 10, 1993.

B.

Documents of the Onslaught

9

"Book Burning" at Wellesley College

by Leo W. Bertley and Winston Nicholls
Afro-Canadian (Montreal)
May 1993

Founded in the 1870's, Wellesley College is a four-year, Liberal Arts educational institution for women situated in the town of the same name in the State of Massachusetts.

This college, with an enrollment of approximately 2200 students, of which number approximately 140 are of African descent, is consistently ranked high among Liberal Arts colleges in the U.S.A.

More often than not, Wellesley heads the list of women's colleges, while it usually places among the first five or six colleges overall. There can be little doubt that Wellesley is regarded as a prestigious school.

Disappointing News

Unfortunately, however, some news emanating from Wellesley recently has been both bad and disappointing. If only a portion of the information this paper has received is correct, the news is sad, and the situation is unworthy of any academic institution, to say nothing about one claiming to be an institution of higher learning.

The controversy at Wellesley College is centered around Professor Tony Martin, of the Africana Studies department, and a text he prescribed for his course in African American History. Entitled *The Secret Relationship Between Blacks and Jews*, the book is published by the Historical Research Department of the Nation of Islam.

One of the formidable Marcus Garvey scholars, Dr. Martin is well known around the world for his innumerable scholarly publications, his dynamic lectures, and his deep erudition. Montrealers are more than familiar with his character, personality and scholarship because we have been fortunate enough to have been addressed by him on two occasions in the 1980's.

International Scholar

A Barrister-at-Law, having studied at Gray's Inn, London, England, Dr. Martin was called to the English bar in 1966 and to the bar of Trinidad and Tobago in 1969.

In addition to being a qualified lawyer, this learned professor holds the B.Sc. degree in Economics from the University of Hull, England; an M.A. and Ph.D. in History from Michigan State University. As mentioned above, his publications are innumerable. They are also solid and represent remarkable contributions in their field.

As a result of his outstanding work, Dr. Martin has received numerous awards and honours from institutions and groups in Africa, the Caribbean, England, the U.S.A., and Canada.

Race First

Indeed, on April 17 of this year, a symposium was held at Wellesley College itself in honour of his [twenty years of] contributions to that institution, as well as to mark the seventeenth anniversary of *Race First*, his seminal work on the Rt. Excellent Marcus Garvey and the Universal Negro Improvement Association.

The Secret Relationship Between Blacks and Jews deals with the involvement of some Jews in the transatlantic slave trade, as well as in the horrendous chattel slavery imposed on Africans by Europeans and their descendants. It is a well-researched, well-documented text based heavily on works by Jewish authors.

Certain groups and individuals are so upset over the presence of this book at Wellesley, that they are doing everything, and we mean everything, in their power to have it excluded from the campus. So much for the first amendment of the constitution, academic freedom, freedom of thought, and all the related freedoms, as far as they are concerned!

These groups and individuals have been using the enormous resources at their disposal to condemn and vilify Dr. Martin, as well as to discredit the book.

With the on-campus and off-campus resources available to them, they have been able to influence some others to support their attempt to "burn" this text as well as the professor who introduced it to his students.

Such a development comes as no surprise. After all these years, one gets accustomed to such tactics and the results they produce in the cowardly and unprincipled, as well as in the weak of heart and the bankrupt of soul.

Barbarism and Genocide

Up to this point, as far as we are aware, Dr. Martin's critics have not produced any convincing evidence, academic, intellectual, or otherwise, to show why the book is unsuitable as a text in African American Studies.

In an interview, Dr. Martin explained that the involvement of other major religious groups, including Christians and Muslims, in both the trans-Atlantic slave trade and chattel slavery which was imposed on Africans by Europeans and their descendants, is well known because of the many works on the subject. In fact, it is difficult to enumerate the number of texts, articles, and the like dealing with those forms of barbarism and genocide.

Until the appearance of *The Secret Relationship Between Blacks and Jews*, however, the part played in that monstrous holocaust of Africans by people professing to be members of the Jewish faith has largely been unknown. It was, indeed, a well kept secret.

Why the Difference?

One interesting feature, Dr. Martin explained, is that Jewish scholars have written about the subject long before the appearance of this book. Yet, however, their works have been ignored, or buried, and the topic placed under a ban, as it were.

With the publication of this book, the subject has been put before the public, and in a manner that they can understand.

Besides, it is very difficult to suppress this text completely, and it is available.

As Dr. Martin has observed, for centuries books have been written about the participation of Christians and Muslims in the slave trade and in chattel slavery. Yet, such works have not been condemned as anti-Christian or anti-Muslim. Why, therefore, Dr. Martin asks, is it anti-Semitic for scholars and others to examine the role played by Jews in this sordid business?

Demonstrate Weakness

This question is particularly relevant because "Jews were indeed involved in every aspect of the African slave trade," Professor Martin remarked. They invested, for example, in the Dutch West India Company, that notorious slave-trading "multinational" corporation, and they were "major slave importers and dealers in places such as Curaçao, Brazil, and Barbados."

All this information is contained in *The Secret Relationship Between Blacks and Jews* which, as Dr. Martin keeps reminding his detractors, as well as those who condemn the book, is based heavily on Jewish sources. Are those Jews who recorded such information anti-Semitic as well?

The illustrious professor has declared that he is more than willing to listen to those who could demonstrate that the information in the text is incorrect, and/or that the book is not well-researched and documented. So far, however, that type of criticism, which one would expect at least from individuals pretending to be academics, has been in very short supply.

Extortion is Extortion

In its stead, one encounters name calling, mindless abuse, irrational association between the text and the Nazi German holocaust, and even with the Palestine Liberation Organization, Abu Nidal and Shamas. Surely, one has a right to expect more from those who would criticize a book and a professor, as well as from those who claim to be scholars.

This form of extortion, used far too frequently, is clearly unacceptable. Fortunately, it no longer has the effect that it once had because more and more individuals are seeing it for what it is: a crude form of whitemail, intended to stifle debate and terrorize scholars and others into silence on certain topics.

If one has problems with a subject, one should debate the subject on its merit. Resort to cheap emotionalism and terroristic tactics is no substitute for rational debate and discussion. Furthermore, people of principle are not cowed into submission by such tactics.

Afraid of the Truth?

As is usually the case in situations such as these, the attempt to "ban the text" and prevent individuals from reading it has had the opposite effect. In fact, *The Afro-Canadian* has been informed that sales of the book have gone up geometrically at Wellesley College and elsewhere since the matter broke out into the open.

This shows that attempts to kill the message usually serve to give it further exposure and, therefore, to strengthen it. This simple fact, demonstrated since time immemorial, should long have been obvious to all, but especially to those who are behaving in such a barbaric and unprincipled manner towards Dr. Tony Martin and *The Secret Relationship Between Blacks and Jews.*

The book should be allowed to stand or fall on its merits, or demerits. Attempting to suppress it merely serves to suggest that its detractors have something to hide. They are afraid of the truth.

We sincerely hope that failure on the part of such individuals to kill the message does not lead them to try to kill the messenger.

10

Letters

Support Letters – Black

June 3, 1993

Peace and blessings unto you, Dr. Martin,

Your recent unforgettable interview with WPFW's Loren Love evinced your formidable scholarship, bulldog tenacity, and high moral resolve. Clearly these traits are vital to one who would throw off the shackles of oppression and defy the intimidating constraints of academic and political correctness in a determined quest for the truth. Unfortunately, there are those who perceive Truth as their mortal enemy and frenetically seek to ferret out and destroy her most ardent pursuers. We see this gruesome phenomenon burgeoning on and off campus across this troubled nation. But let the truth ring out though the heavens may fall!

Would be that your baying detractors, Dr. Martin, could emulate your sterling performance. Please be assured that decent people all over this country hold you and your intrepid colleagues who are maligned, pilloried, libeled, and slandered, for merely seeking and telling the truth, in the highest esteem. We regard you as the last faint glimmer of hope for this immoral, amoral, and decadent society. Please forward a copy of BROADSIDE. Good luck and God bless.

[Washington, DC.]

cc: President, Wellesley College
    Chairman, Africana Studies Department
    Loren Love, WPFW, D.C.

April 8, 1993

Dear Tony,

After reading and hearing about the recent attacks leveled against you by Zionist and other reactionary forces, I felt compelled to send you this brief expression of support. The courage you've demonstrated in speaking the truth, in the face of such a tremendous onslaught of political conservatism, academic Eurocentrism and Zionist machinations, is very inspiring and reminiscent of the kind of battles waged by Asantewa, Turner, Tubman, Garvey, Barnett, Malcolm, Hamer, Nkrumah, and countless others on your behalf. For this reason, alone, I, personally, am very grateful.

Like so many others, I have enthusiastically followed your work over the years, and have gained from it immensely. As the world's leading scholar on Garvey, you have ensured that at least one of our heroes of monumental importance will not suffer, as others have, at the hands of European custodialship and bourgeois – regardless of race – scholarship. Moreover, it is imperative that we always stand united when someone who represents the intellectual, cultural, and political integrity of our people is attacked by the backward, albeit powerful, forces of the Zionist movement.

For these reasons, Tony, please know that if there is anything I can do in support of your efforts at Wellesley College, I am just a phone call away. Meanwhile, take care, stay alert, and be strong.

Fraternally,

Michael Williams
Director
African American Studies
Simmons College, Boston

June 3, 1993

Dear Dr. Martin,

By chance, the other day, I was lucky enough to hear a very inspiring interview granted by you to WOL radio, 1450AM, here in DC. The topic concerned your confrontation with the Jewish establishment and in turn, Wellesley College.

It's exciting to hear a determined black man with a plan for change. I pray that God helps you and helps those of us willing to take the risk of siding with you.

During your interview, you mentioned a newsletter, "The Broadside." Please, send me a copy(ies) so that I can continue to remain informed and able to contribute knowledgeably.

[Laurel, Maryland]

May 14, 1993

President Nannerl Keohane,
Wellesley College
Wellesley, Mass. 02181

Dear President Keohane,

Unfortunately, the uproar over Professor Tony Martin's use of the book on the Jewish community's involvement in the slave trade has reached Chicago. The information in the media states that Wellesley College's administration has censored Professor Martin for using the book without allowing him to defend himself, and that there are maneuvers being made to review his tenure.

From afar, it appears that you have impugned the integrity of a tenured professor without due process. And, I have never heard of a tenured professor being reviewed for the use of one book in a course he is teaching.

The question that I have is, were Jews involved in the slave trade? And, if they were, so what? It was the most profitable enterprise that Judeo-Christian Western Civilization was involved in up to that time.

I hope that the administration does not dismiss Professor Martin from his position, because it would indicate that censorship is alive and well on a college campus with a reputation for liberal thought. And once this kind of restriction takes hold it is so scary that it might continue until we have reverted to the historical period in America when Black men and women were not allowed to read or write. I hope that liberal education is not coming to this.

[Chicago, Illinois]

cc: Professor Tony Martin

May 16, 1993

Ms. Nancy Kolodny
Dean
Wellesley College
Wellesley, MA 02181

Dear Ms. Kolodny,
You were quoted in the *New York Times* as saying that Professor Tony Martin "was misusing his constitutional right" when he used the book *The Secret Relationship Between Blacks and Jews* in his class. As was recently demonstrated in the case of Professor Leonard Jeffries, the constitutional right to free speech cannot be abridged by the administration of a university. Professor Tony Martin has every right to exercise his rights to free speech and academic freedom, even if that is offensive to certain groups.

I am quite concerned about the role of Wellesley in all this. Instead of the college defending the right to free speech and academic freedom for an experienced and tenured professor, the college is fanning the flames of intolerance, hatred and fear.

The current situation could have been a real opportunity for growth for Wellesley. If the administration had encouraged it, it could have led to debate, discussion, sharing, collaboration, research, and mutual respect. In short, the Wellesley community could have conducted itself like an institution of higher learning. But instead we have an ugly, mainly one-sided, mudslinging contest.

I support Professor Tony Martin's constitutional right to free speech and hope that the Wellesley community will begin to do the same.

[Brooklyn, NY]

cc: Tony Martin

May 18, 1993

Dear Tony,
I have been following the recent controversy relating to your teaching of *The Secret Relationship Between Blacks and Jews*. I recently read the first issue of Broadside, and wanted you to know that I

respect your strong responses to these unfounded attacks on your academic freedom. If there is anything I can concretely do in support of you, please let me know.

Tony, your commitment to the African cause is deeply appreciated by your community and the ancestors. The ancestors will continue to guide your path.

[Professor, State University of New York]

May 14, 1993

President
Wellesley College
Wellesley, Mass. 02181

Dear President,

I am writing in support of Professor Martin of the Department of Africana Studies. Professor Martin is not a racist or being irresponsible in his behavior. He is attempting to introduce literature into his classes that will offer a balance. We have all been victims of institutions that have endlessly promoted European history at the expense of every other culture. These institutions have gone so far as to distort history. This entire nation has suffered as a result.

I remember sitting in classrooms being told that my history started with the slave trade and that I was nothing before that. I thank God that I was blessed with African-American teachers, some who knew differently, and a Jewish grade school principal, Dr. Shapiro, who taught us children differently. He decorated our school walls and classrooms with pictures and other supporting materials that supported my rich cultural heritage.

Dr. Martin is being harassed by those persons who are afraid of the truth. Only the truth will set this nation free!

[New York, NY]

May 14, 1993

President Nannerl Keohane
Wellesley College
Office of the President
106 Central Street
Wellesley, MA 02181

Dear Madame President,

I am writing to express my profound dismay with the firestorm currently surrounding Professor Tony Martin. There are three issues which have been obfuscated by gratuitous name calling and invidious race baiting.

First, one expects the university to provide an intellectual milieu conducive to the dispassionate examination of information. Such critical analysis cannot be performed when certain books are arbitrarily excluded from a reading list. Scholarship demands the critique of knowledge; that criticism cannot be conducted when some books are declared off limits.

Second, let us be clear on the point that anti-Semitism is repugnant, reprehensible, intolerable and should never be condoned. But let us not diminish the validity of anti-Semitism by branding as anti-Semitic those people we simply disagree with. Dr. Martin's selection of a particular book does not, *ipso facto* make him anti-Semitic. After all, the Bible is opposed to homosexuality. Does that mean that if Dr. Martin puts the Bible on a reading list, he is therefore anti-Gay?

Third, without positing any sort of conspiracy theory, one needs to be aware of a trend within academia towards censuring African intellectuals. Consider Dr. Fred Dube of the Stony Brook campus who was harassed and dismissed because he challenged his class to contemplate whether Zionism was a form of racism. Consider Dr. Jeffries who achieved infamy and was demoted from chairmanship at C.U.N.Y. because of an allegedly anti-Semitic speech in Albany. Now consider Dr. Martin who is being smeared as anti-Semitic because of his choice of book.

In all three cases opponents are not interested in evaluating the substance of the positions of the professors. Opponents are not interested in exploring whether there is any factual basis to the positions of the scholars. Opponents are not interested in reviewing the pedagogical content or merit of the curriculum. What is heard most loudly are the insistent demands to dismiss African intellectuals because of their allegedly anti-Semitic views. This trivializes, demeans and perverts the legitimate meaning of anti-Semitism.

This also subverts the role of a university. Unarguably, a university must maintain its hallowed tradition of being the marketplace of ideas. The university must remain a place where ideas, no matter how far-fetched, are debated dispassionately. This is the only rational method for allowing good ideas to drive out bad; in this manner we get closer to the truth. Contemporaries of Copernicus would have considered his seminal ideas far-fetched; of course no one thinks so today.

In the case of Dr. Martin this nonsense has gone too far. Should we take it to its logical conclusions, then Dr. Martin may be afraid to assign *The Merchant of Venice*, because of apprehensions of being branded anti-Semitic. Indeed one can easily make a plausible, yet superficial case that Shakespeare was anti-Semitic because of his characterization of Shylock. Dr. Martin's persecution will undoubtedly have a chilling effect, as African educators are forced to select reading material on the basis of its acceptability to certain interest groups.

No one can impugn the impeccable scholarship of Dr. Martin. His prodigious output is manifestly self-evident. Neither can his well deserved international reputation be destroyed by crude and groundless charges. But if Dr. Martin's reputation is threatened and his character slandered, what hope is there for lesser untenured lights? It is therefore incumbent on Wellesley's leadership to loudly, publicly and unambiguously support Dr. Martin. At risk is a pivotal principle; it is vital that we now support a principled position. The stakes are academic freedom and we need to know, which side are you on Nan?

[New York, NY]

cc: Dean Nancy Kolodny
     Professor Selwyn Cudjoe
     Professor Tony Martin

April 7, 1993

Letters
The Boston Globe
Morrissey Blvd.
Boston, Mass.

Dear Sir or Madam,
   The Wellesley professor being attacked by the very powerful and rich Jewish groups, especially the Anti-Defamation League, is correct in saying that the "anti-semitic" charge is used to suppress free speech. The proof is in 50 years of escalating Jewish violence against the Palestinian and other people of the Mid-East, that's been nixed for criticism. Even Jews who dare to speak up are called "anti-semitic."
   I don't know about the Nation of Islam's charge about Jewish money and the slave trade, but it warrants investigation not suppression. According to the *Encyclopedia Brittanica* (under Rothschild) the Rothschild family "controlled European finance" a few centuries later, so it's not so far-fetched.
   What also adds up is these powerful Jewish groups' desire to censor education. They already control Congress through the AIPAC (American Israel Public Affairs Committee), seeing to it that no Congressman survives who votes against Israeli interests.

                    Yours truly,

                    A citizen
                    [Boston, Massachusetts]

P.S. The letter is unsigned because of Jewish terroristic activity in the U.S.
   cc: Anthony Martin
        Selwyn Cudjoe, Chair, Africana Studies
        Nannerl O. Keohane, President, Wellesley College

[*The* Boston Globe *naturally did not publish this letter.*]

May 24, 1993

Dear Tony,
   Greetings. I hope this letter will find you in the best physical and emotional state. I was driving to work one day last week, and was surprised to hear that you are a racist. I see you're giving Wellesley hell! Fight on! The truth is always hard to swallow for people who are not of color. Were you to publish a text that declared the inferiority of our people, you would be praised. I am ashamed to say that I attended an institution that could support such narrow minded "scholars." I should have realized that once Wellesley professors openly supported the notion that Cleopatra was not a woman of color, that "education" is not always a measure of one's intelligence. It is shameful that those who appear to be so advanced, are actually far behind.
   I pray for the struggle at Wellesley. There are so many influential minds that are being led blindly into a tunnel of racial blindness. Keep up the good work. I am and always will be one of your devout followers (smile). Please let me know when you will be in the New York area. I was told that you recently gave a speech at the Harriet Tubman School. I was unfortunately unaware at the time.
   Thank you for your inspiration. Thanks to you, I have become a more enlightened woman. Thank you for molding my mind. Again, keep fighting!

[Wellesley College alumna, '91, Queens, NY]

April 29, 1993

Dear Dr. Martin,
   On the aforementioned date, I read an article by the *New York Times News Service*. The article was in regards to your use of the book – *The Secret Relationship Between Blacks and Jews* which was prepared by the Nation of Islam. I immediately decided to write you this letter in support of your courageous and responsible attempt to disseminate the truth to your students. I've read all your published books on Marcus Garvey and treasure *Race First*. Your title as the Marcus Garvey Scholar is well deserved and well earned!

I also have the cassette tape of a lecture you delivered on Garvey in Dallas some time ago. It was your scholarship that pulled my coat to Marcus Garvey and the Universal Negro Improvement Association. I support and applaud your choice of books to disseminate the truth one hundred percent.

I read *The Secret Relationship Between Blacks and Jews* when it was first released and found it to be credible. As an Afrikan man born in Amerika, I can't thank you enough for your contribution to Afrikan minds. It must be a terribly bitter pill to swallow for these so-called European Jews. I have never heard them substantiate their charge of anti-Semitism; be it against you, Dr. Leonard Jeffries, Dr. Yosef ben-Jochannan, Dr. John Henrik Clarke, or even Louis Farrakhan. European Jewish scholars admit that the Jews played an active and strong role in the Afrikan slave trade. They were involved in all facets of slavery involving Afrikans. They owned the ships, financed the slave hunting voyages, controlled and operated the slave auction blocks on the east coast of the United States, bought Afrikans, raped Afrikan women, etc....The evidence against the Jews is overwhelmingly conclusive. The dean of the college, Nancy Kolodny was quoted as saying that you have the right to use the book even though it is "hateful." What is hateful about the book? Afrikans are anti-semitic when we wake up to the major FRAUD that was perpetrated against our people. From the Spingarn brothers of the NAACP to the present day, Jews have always tried to pass themselves off as paternal benefactors for Afrikan people. White women and Jews were the ones who benefited from the civil rights movement of the sixties. What you are doing has nothing to do with hatred or anti-semitism. The European Jews are not the original Semites of biblical history in the first place. They converted to Judaism in the eighth century according to Arthur Koestler, who is a European Jew and author of the book *The Thirteenth Tribe.* Koestler termed the current Jews passing themselves off as descendants of the biblical Hebrews as one of the biggest frauds in history. Michael Bradley's book, *The Chosen People of the Caucasus,* shed more light on the issue. I must stress that racial hatred is a totally illogical course of action. No right thinking person of reasonable intelligence should subscribe to racial hatred. European historians or intellectuals must think that they are the only ones that can disseminate information or bring forth revelations. I once again would like to commend your actions and encourage you to continue your efforts in awakening Afrikan minds. HANG IN THERE! – You're not struggling alone.

[Richardson, Texas]

May 28, 1993

Greetings,

The survival of a nation depends upon the obedience of that particular nation's covenant by each and every individual member of the nation. Although all are not aware, the descendants of Africa have a "Holy Covenant of the Asiatic Nation." This covenant established by the Holy Prophet Noble Drew Ali, founder of the Moorish Science Temple of America, includes all those so-called people of color, but is specifically, in my interpretation, for the descendants of Africa. Being that I am presently incarcerated, I cannot offer much assistance to you my brother as our covenant would require me to do in this time of adversity if you will; however, I can and will make every brother here aware of what happened to you with hopes that they will arm themselves with the facts to fight with.

I taped your interview with sister Loren Cress Love and I was enlightened by your assertions. In your responses to her questions you demonstrated the greatest fears of Europeans who wish ignorance would remain our friend. What has happened to you and Dr. Jeffries only supports what Dr. Na'im Akbar says in his book, *Visions for Black Men*, that when one stands up in this country and in many places in this world as a true African – upright, independent, and fearless – he must be prepared for attack and all out war. Nevertheless, I am convinced that in order for freedom and justice to reach fruition here on earth, it is going to take the contributions of African men like yourself who have courage enough for truth.

I've lived an alienated life caught up in the carnal customs and ideas of others. However, slowly I've awakened to another side of life and the infinity of the mind. I'm tired of being a contributionless, unproductive individual. Now is the time for me to free myself from slavery. This state of mind is possible because of, most importantly, the influence Prophet Noble Drew Ali's teachings have had on me and the courageousness of brothers like you. As far as I'm concerned, you are due much honor and should take your place in history as one of the noble men who took a stand for what's right.

I would like to further my understanding of this matter; therefore, would you please send me a copy of "Broadside No. 1." Furthermore, if there is any information you could send that would further my understanding of African-American history I would greatly appreciate it.   At the present time, I am unable to compensate you for your service to us all. But in the event I am able to, would gladly do so. May the great God of the universe protect you.

[Hagerstown, Maryland]

P.S. Please find enclosed a self-addressed envelope for a copy of "Broadside No. 1."

May 20, 1993

Dear Professor Martin,

I am a brother incarcerated at the Old Walpole Prison now called Cedar Junction.

I have been following the scattered media coverage of your socio-politic-economic-historical views which have brought about some controversy, especially within the Jewish community. Secondly, on this day I have had the privilege to watch you interact with other dignitaries regarding the issue of Leonard Jeffries, I believe. I need not go any farther by saying that the brothers and I here at Cedar Junction are in complete agreement with your analysis of the importance of Afrocentrism, moreso, the significance of enlightening African-Americans to the true history of our ancestors.

Reflectively, I read [a *Boston Herald*] article by Don Feder, an individual who I personally have great disdain for, which depicts you as a multiculturalist promoting anti-semitism. Aside from the rhetorical nonsense, I am very much interested in obtaining the two books indicated within the article – *The Secret Relationship Between*

Blacks and Jews and *The Protocols of the Elders of Zion.* Both books cannot be found in our prison library. Therefore, I am respectfully asking if you can provide me with a copy of both books so that I can share them with other brothers by making zerox copies....

Lastly, in the near future we will be sending an invitation to you to come out to the prison and speak with the brothers in a forum type setting. Personally, I would like to continue my correspondence with you regarding issues which crop up within our prison group. Until then, take care and stay strong in the struggle.

[Walpole, Massachusetts]

May 25, 1993

Professor Anthony Martin,

I hope that my words meet you in the best of health and positive frame of mind. From the onset, let me just say that I am incarcerated at Walpole prison. I had the pleasure of seeing you on public television. You impressed me that you stuck to your position.

Professor Martin, check this out – I am sick and tired of hearing people of the Jewish race/religion reiterating time and time again that they are friends of the Black man. Yet, not only do they torture and oppress brown people (in *stolen land* which they received via the good people of England: Churchill's Crew). Yet, they blow up the homes of innocent people in Israel, the Palestinians, killing children, etc.... But more importantly, they sell weapons to every country that has money to spend – including the South African government.

It bothers the hell out of me, as it should you, that even on shows like "Urban Update," they limit stories covering international news about people of color. Professor Martin, remember that show "South Africa Now?" It just seems strange to me that we must continue to pretend that Israel is a "democratic state." Yet they have the most powerful lobbyists in Washington, D.C. *Can we forget Sharon?*

Professor Martin, I have been in isolation since 1988. Materials are hard for me to get. If you could send me something, I can study my lessons and keep up with my studies. They do not allow hard cover books in here.

Professor Martin, I heard about the propaganda they tried to use to kill your character but you stayed strong, *AND I RESPECT THAT TO THE FULLEST*....Don't compromise with them ever.

Take Care and Stay Strong.
Peace, Progress, and
Prosperity,

[Walpole, Massachusetts]

Support Letters – White

April 29, 1993

Dear Professor Martin,

I'm sure the last thing you need is to hear from some semi-literate Irishman from a [_____] ghetto, but I had to write when I saw a newspaper article about the furor over your use of a book.

You are a very brave man. You have to know the power that will be leveled against you. I haven't read the book – never heard of it. But now, I'm married to a New York...woman...and I love my in-laws. I used to really support Israel but couldn't understand how they could treat Palestinians the way they do. I'm not anti-Semitic, I'm sure you're not either, nor is Louis Farrakhan. But using true information *is* an attack on powerful interests. Jewish people in this country have incredible power and don't hesitate to use it to further *their* goals. Nothing stops them – not morality, not truth, not even America's best interests. (I'm not a flag waver, but I respect the people of this country.)

They – A.I.P.A.C., B'nai B'rith, J.D.L., etc., will beat you into the ground. You won't win, only morally. You must already have a tough backbone but you'll need more. Make contacts with everyone you can, (obviously not fascists or hate-mongers), because you'll need all the help you can get. Maybe that's something you're unaccustomed to – relying on others. Your opponents will manage every dirty trick imaginable and then some and you'll be out on your ear. You need to plan and outreach immediately.

I have read a lot of books lately about Jewish influence in the U.S.A. A very mainstream, well published book is [Paul Findley's] *They Dare to Speak Out*. I've enclosed a few pages. Try and get it. Contact the academic people mentioned along with the American Library Association.

I wish you all the luck in the world.

[____]

April 25, 1993

Dear Mr. Martin,

In light of the recent uproar over your presentation of the text, *The Secret Relationship Between Blacks and Jews*, *The Galenstone* would like to offer you the opportunity to express your views in an open letter to the college community.

The issue has, as you well know, drawn many heated opinions. We at *The Galenstone* were greatly surprised that the *Wellesley News* would not publish your own letter of defense to the accusations lobbied against both yourself and the text. This seems to be an astonishing display of favoritism. We were impressed with the initiative that led you to print your views in a newsletter of your own designing. Now we would like to offer you another forum, in our final issue, due to be published in the first week of May.

Due to the time constraints of our publishing schedule, we must receive your letter by Thursday, April 29. *Letters must be no longer than 1400 words, and we do reserve the right to edit the text.* A telephone call to notify us if you intend to contribute a letter would be greatly appreciated.

We are very interested in presenting your views to the college community at large. We hope that you will take advantage of this forum.

[Editor-in-Chief, *The Galenstone*, Wellesley College]

Jewish Hate Mail

[Punctuation, grammar, etc. are reproduced exactly as in the originals.]

[No Date]

Filthy Nigger Ape,

Yeah, So what. Jews financed the slave trade. I plead guilty. Who gives a shit except liberal, self hating nigger ass kissers.

As for me, I hate dirty nigger apes. hopes Aids destroys your accursed race, I'm glad 23 million apes died on slave ships etc.

Filthy nigger simian pigs have destroyed America with their rapes, looting murder, neanderthal conduct – And Tony coon – youse chimps smells.

Niggers have no redeeming value and should be castrated, sent back to Africa or drowned. I hate niggers to my very bone marrow.

Not all Jews debate apes. Some of us want them all to die.

NEVER AGAIN!

We are Jews who hate Coons.

[New York, NY]

NIGGERS VS WATER BUFFALO

1. HUGE LIPS
2. HUGE NOSTRILS
3. BLACK EYES
4. WHITE NIGHT TEETH
5. ALL THE ABOVE

ANS: 5 ALL THE ABOVE

WHITE JESUS AND 13 WHITE APOSTLES AS ARE ALL WHITES A SUPERIOR PEOPLE.
GENESIS 9-25-27

"CURSED BE THE NIGGER CANAAN: A SLAVE OF
SLAVES SHALL HE BE TO HIS BROTHERS FOR ALL
ETERNITY. GOD ENLARGE JAPHETH AND SHEM
AND LET CANAAN AND HIS ISSUE FOR ALL TIME
BE THEIR SLAVES."
SO SAID JESUS

[*Signed by someone allegedly from Boynton Beach, Florida. He included a
telephone number.*]

American Jewish Committee–
Letter on Lani Guinier

[*Martin Goldman, deputy executive director, American Jewish Committee,
New England Region, refers here to the 1993 Clinton administration
nomination of law professor Lani Guinier as Assistant Attorney General
for Civil Rights. President Bill Clinton aborted the nomination before
Senate confirmation hearings could take place. The following quotation
can shed some light on the situation –*

"*As in the case of Spelman College president Johnetta Cole, another
African-American woman and potential Clinton appointee smeared by the
right in the early weeks of the Administration, this witch hunt
unfortunately finds willing collaborators among those who ought to be in
her court – some leading Jewish organizations. Staff members from both
the Anti-Defamation League and the American Jewish Congress have been
chanting 'quota' in mesmerized unison.*"
- Bruce Shapiro, "Getting Guinier," *The Nation*, May 31, 1993, p.
724.]

from the desk of...

Martin S. Goldman

June 4, 1993

Dear Tony,

And now...[sic] I suppose you will be blaming us (the Jews) for
the demise of Professor Lani Guinier. Of course, the withdrawal of

her nomination by President Clinton could hardly have had anything to do with her published writing and "scholarship."

But when you blame the Jews for this one, be very careful. Professor Guinier's mother is Jewish – which technically makes her half-Jewish. But, in our tradition, makes her completely Jewish. Of course, you can resolve your dilemma by blaming that half of Professor Lani Guinier that is Jewish for the African Slave Trade. You will, undoubtedly, be able to ably resolve your dilemma.

Marty Goldman
American Jewish Committee

A Friendly Jewish Voice

May 10, 1993

Dear Tony,

Let me start off by completely solidarizing myself (and the Committee to Stop Israel's Arms Traffic with South Africa) with you and your absolute right to use the Nation of Islam's *The Secret Relationship Between Blacks and Jews* in your class. Academic freedom means the right to use any and all texts, if they will bring some light on your subject, Black history. Furthermore, politically, the day is long past when the Black community will tolerate any whites telling any Black what book they can or cannot read, or use in teaching.

As you know, I reviewed the book for the [New York] *Amsterdam News* (Sept. 26, Oct. 3 and 10, 1992). I said then, and say now that

> The only way to judge it is to look at it exactly as educated readers look at any nonfiction. Frequently, authors' philosophical failings cause them to misinterpret some aspects of their specialty while doing an adequate job on other facets of their topic. The question is whether readers can learn from the book even with its failings. Using that criterion, if I were a professor, I'd give it a B.

As Richard Muhammad, the managing editor of the *Final Call*, the Nation of Islam's paper, wrote, in his interview with you (May 10, 1993), "Neither the book nor Dr. Martin claim Jews dominated the American slave trade, nor was the text chosen as an attack on Jews." In fact the least controversial part of the book is its description of the magnitude of Jewish involvement in the slave trade. The NOI's scholars cited numerous Jewish writers on this.

I believe that a large part of the problem lies in the fact that the overwhelming majority of today's American Jews are descendants of Ashkenazi Jews from central and eastern Europe, who arrived here after the Civil War. Most of them know nothing about the prior Sephardic colonization here, much less the Sephardic role in South America and the Caribbean. Therefore their automatic attitude is to say something like, "Yes, Jews held Black slaves, but why focus on that?" The reason is that those Sephardic Jews played a significant part in the slave trade, and not to study their role would be the same as not studying the role of the Dutch or any other major factor in that traffic. God, they say, is in the details.

To understand their role, it is necessary to know some Portuguese history. As many people know, the Spanish crown gave the Jews a choice in 1492, convert to Catholicism or be exiled. But the Portuguese king decided that it would be foolish to expel such an important part of his country's merchants. Instead, he forcibly converted all the Jews. Naturally most of them continued to think of themselves as Jews. But once he sprinkled some holy water on them, he proceeded to do business with them, as usual. The *Encyclopedia Judaica* article on Brazil tells the story:

> In 1502 a consortium of New Christians headed by Fernando de Noronha obtained from King Manuel I of Portugal a concession to colonize and exploit the newly discovered land....A large number of the 120 *engenhos* [sugar plantations with mills – LB] that existed on Brazil in the year 1600 belonged to New Christians, many of whom were also administrators....The majority secretly observed Jewish rites....Brazil had about 50,000 European inhabitants in 1624, a high percentage of whom were New Christians.

The Dutch took northeastern Brazil from the Portuguese in 1630 and, again, according to the *Encyclopedia Judaica*,

> [M]any Marranos (Portuguese for secret Jews)...happy to be able to give up their double life, were circumcised and became professing Jews....Jews...were largely engaged in the slave trade. The import of Negro slaves from Africa was a monopoly of the West India

Company, which sold them at public auction for cash. Jews purchased the slaves and resold them at great profit (on credit, payable at the next sugar harvest) to the owners of the plantations.

By 1645, Jews were "about 50%" of the European population of Dutch Brazil. But the Portuguese reconquered the Dutch settlement at Pernambuco in 1654 and the open Jews had to leave with the Dutch:

> The majority left for Amsterdam, but some sailed to Caribbean Islands (Curaçao, Barbados, etc.) where they are believed to have introduced the sugar plant and the sugar industry.

It isn't necessary to quote further. Anyone seriously interested in the topic can read the *Encyclopedia Judaica* articles on all the European colonies on and in the Caribbean. There they will see for themselves, from Jewish scholarly sources, that Jews played a major role in slavery in that region. If they read further, they will see that the first American Jews in this country migrated here from their strong economic base in the Caribbean. Because they came here relatively late, and in small numbers, Jews never were as important here in the slave traffic as in Brazil or the Caribbean. Nevertheless, they were most definitely a major factor in Newport, Rhode Island, where Aaron Lopez was the "leading Merchant and her largest taxpayer" (*Encyclopedia Judaica*, Vol. 11).

Slavery is ancient and all three monotheistic faiths condoned it. The Jewish role in slavery is important because wherever they were allowed to live they made up a significant proportion of the merchant class. But it must also be understood that nowhere and at no time in the entire period of the Black slave trade were the Jews the dominant political or even economic power. Those Jews who took part in the crime of slavery were everywhere a minority of the slaveholding and slave trading class. The vast majority of slaveholders and traders in the Americas were Christians and the vast majority in North Africa and the Middle East were Muslims.

Nevertheless, it is disgraceful that you should be attacked for discussing the Jewish role in that traffic, and in using the Nation of Islam's book. Who thinks that anyone would have complained if you had dealt with the role of Christians or Muslims in the African holocaust? And it is particularly odious that the Anti-Defamation

League should be among your tormentors. Anyone reading the papers now knows that the organization is a non-stop spy outfit, "investigating" innumerable Black groups, and the progressive camp in general.

If I or the CSIATSA can be of further assistance to you, do not hesitate to call on us.

In solidarity,

Lenni Brenner
(for the CSIATSA)

[This is a good example of the type of principled dialogue that can take place between Blacks and Jews, even where both sides do not agree on every detail. While I agree with most of what Brenner has to say, I would argue that the question of whether Jews were the dominant political or economic power overall in any particular place is largely irrelevant. This particular debate is about their role in the slave trade, and in the slave trade they were a dominant factor (Brenner allows a "significant" factor) in Brazil, Curaçao and elsewhere. Consider the testimony of the Jewish historian, Seymour B. Liebman – "They [Jews] came with ships carrying African blacks to be sold as slaves. The traffic in slaves was a royal monopoly, and the Jews were often appointed as agents for the Crown in their sale....[They] were the largest ship chandlers in the entire Caribbean region, where the shipping business was mainly a Jewish enterprise....The ships were not only owned by Jews, but were manned by Jewish crews and sailed under the command of Jewish captains." (Seymour B. Liebman, New World Jewry, 1493-1825: Requiem for the Forgotten, *New York, 1982, pp. 170, 183).*

Or consider the Jewish historian Herbert I. Bloom – "The Christian inhabitants [of Brazil] were envious because the Jews owned some of the best plantations in the river valley of Pernambuco and were among the leading slave-holders and slave traders in the colony." (Herbert I. Bloom, "A Study of Brazilian Jewish History, 1623-1654...," Publications of the American Jewish Historical Society, *Vol. 33 (1934), p. 63. Or consider Bloom again, this time on Suriname –"Slave trade was one of the most important Jewish activities here as elsewhere in the colonies." (Bloom,* The Economic Activities of the Jews of Amsterdam in the Seventeenth and Eighteenth Centuries *(Port Washington, NY [1969, c1937] p. 159).*

Again, even though I agree that Jewish involvement in African slavery in the United States may not have been as overwhelming as in Brazil, one must not forget that the Jewish historian Lee Soltow found a 75% slave ownership among Southern Jewish households in 1830, compared with only a 36% slaveholding for all slave households – Ira Rosenwaike, On the Edge of Greatness: A Portrait of American Jewry in the Early National Period *(Cincinnati, 1985, p. 66). (I am indebted to the Historical Research Department, Boston, for these references).*

The question of North African slavery does not seem to belong here, since it was an equal opportunity business, with victims of all colours. Even here, though, Jews were "for a few centuries at least [from medieval times] among the world's premier slave traders...." – see the Jewish historian Harold D. Brackman, "The Ebb and Flow of Conflict: A History of Black-Jewish Relations Through 1900, Part I," Ph.D. dissertation, UCLA, 1977, p. 41.

As to whether Christians or Muslims would have complained had I dealt with their role in African slavery – the question is not a hypothetical one. I have taught their involvement (especially that of Christians, as more relevant to the courses I teach), for over two decades. No Quaker, Roman Catholic, Moravian or Baptist has sought to have me fired for doing so. That singular distinction rests with the American Jewish Committee, Anti-Defamation League, American Jewish Congress, the Hillel Foundation, the Jewish Community Relations Council and their hydra-headed co-thinkers – T.M.]

My Letter to the *Boston Globe*

[The *Boston Globe* did not consider this letter fit to print.]

April 11, 1993

The Editor
Boston Globe

Dear Sir:
    Anthony Flint's article on my teaching of *The Secret Relationship Between Blacks and Jews* at Wellesley College raises several interesting points. His suggestion that the book accuses Jews of being "genetically prone to enslaving others" is entirely without

foundation. This assertion (which Flint was simply repeating from earlier stories) would seem to be an invention of the Anti-Defamation League.

Henry Gates' assertion that "Jews did not 'run' the slave trade" is equally perplexing. Gates is here jousting with a man of straw. While Jews were in fact dominant elements in the slave trade in Brazil, Curaçao, and elsewhere, Flint is correct when he says that "Jews played a vital [though not necessarily dominant] role" in the trade in the United States.

When Alan Dershowitz calls the book "a political-religious-ethnic-tract" I must conclude that he has never seen it, let alone read it. The book is a scholarly monograph, and based overwhelmingly on the work of Jewish scholars, from whom it quotes liberally. This fact has been strangely absent from recent commentary.

Flint is correct when he says that "Truth is the standard in teaching." The question, though, is, whose truth – that of the slavemaster or that of the slave?

Sincerely,

Tony Martin
Professor

11

Student Voices

Students Protest Call for Contract Review
Wellesley News
May 7, 1993

[Wellesley News] *Editor's note: This was submitted as an open letter to the Anti-Defamation League, American Jewish Committee American Jewish Congress and the Jewish Community Relations Council.*

You have made several allegations regarding Dr. Martin's choice of a particular source towards documenting Jewish involvement in the Trans-Atlantic Slave Trade. While we respect your dissenting opinion, your call to our college trustees and administration to review his contract and tenure status is totally inappropriate and unacceptable.

Here at Wellesley College, we attempt to be as informed and open as possible when facing sensitive issues. The tenure process is an area in which the women of Wellesley have placed much attention. We play a vital role in the career of our professors through Student Evaluation Questionnaires, and we also may write letters of support to the Committee on Faculty Appointments. Our dean, Nancy Kolodny, recently printed a somewhat extensive article in *The Wellesley News* highlighting the tenure process that Wellesley women would be clear as to the criteria set forth by the College.

Wellesley College looks for outstanding scholarship in their instructors – Dr. Martin has published eight books on Marcus Garvey, established the most authoritative, fully documented series in this area, the New Marcus Garvey Library, written dozens of published articles in scholarly journals and is a well-known, well-traveled historian. Wellesley College demands a commitment to service within our community – Dr. Martin has supervised most of the honors theses in his department, worked as chairman of the department almost half of his twenty years here at Wellesley and arranged for students to attend historical and cultural conferences throughout the continental United States and the Caribbean. Wellesley College looks for outstanding teaching abilities – Dr. Martin here again has excelled even Wellesley's high standards with a record of 20 years, strong student support and an obvious concern for developing critical and independent thinking women.

Neither in your April 5 press release nor in the *Boston Globe* article of April 7 did you exhibit any depth of understanding of this process. Your personal opinion regarding our professor's intentions in selecting the assailed "anti-Semitic" text is acceptable, but your paranoid, arrogant and irritated suggestion to criticize his place at Wellesley is an uninformed, irrational and offensive move.

Wellesley women from the White House to the present student body are accustomed to dealing with diverse opinions. But, in the words of our president, Nannerl O. Keohane, "...we owe it to ourselves and our community to know exactly what it is we are tolerating." We, therefore, cannot allow your organizations to place a member of OUR community under siege. You have unfairly attacked him and that is not tolerable behavior for forces who claim to champion "academic conduct."

We believe that here at Wellesley, tenure allows a scholar to further the intellectual growth of and stimulate analytical dialogue among intelligent and capable women. Dr. Martin's uncompromising efforts to fully educate and expose his students to a wider perspective is an excellent example of the traditional Wellesley way of professional mentoring.

LaTrese E. Adkins '93	Caroline Ebanks '95
Nia Higginbothan '93	Nichole R. Phillips '93
Tanya Jarret '95	Thalia V. Shirley '94
Sara E. Miller '96	Diane Holmes '94
Tanisha R. Landry '93	Joy Styles '96
Adriane Williams '96	

Students Claim *News* Lacked Impartiality When Dealing with Controversy

Wellesley News
May 7, 1993

To the Editor:

The purpose of this letter is to express our reactions to the treatment of the Professor Martin "controversy" by *The Wellesley News*. We are concerned Wellesley College students who, for the past few months, have been voiceless. Our aim is to address the biases and the issues we find problematic, in a series of four *Wellesley News* articles concerning this controversy. In our opinion, these issues warrant our time and energy in reaction to *The Wellesley News'* unrelenting pursuit of making them front page news.

In the February 19, 1993 issue of *The Wellesley News*, there are clear and distinct biases. There are four explicit quotes from Professor Martin and seven direct quotes in opposition. Professor Martin is the only one speaking on his behalf, whereas opposing him are: anonymous students, Mary Lefkowitz, Laura Greer, Nancy Kolodny, and Rabbi Ilene Bogosian. There were no quotes from students in the class.

In the same article it is mentioned that the Nation of Islam is "shirking" off its responsibility by assuming authorship of the book *The Secret Relationship Between Blacks and Jews*. We believe the *Wellesley News* has been relaying misinformation to the Wellesley community and beyond. They fail to understand that this book was only *published* by the Nation of Islam. The real authors are unknown.

In the March 10, 1993 *Wellesley News*, there are examples of misinformation. The purpose of the article was to address the discussions concerning Professor Tony Martin's use of the book *The Secret Relationship Between Blacks and Jews* in Academic Council. The article deviates from its original intent. When stating that Professor Martin has to resort to publishing his own newsletter, they neglect to mention why he was forced to publish it in this manner. Professor Martin stated at Academic Council that his reason for seeking another outlet was because *The Wellesley News* would not allow him to voice his opinion, in the way he thought was most appropriate.

In regards to *The Wellesley News* April 1st edition, specifically the "Letter from the desk of Tony Martin" – that is, simply put, *distasteful humor.* We hope that *The Wellesley News* can realize that their little joke was not only an offense to Professor Martin, but also to African American students campus wide. Taking the seriousness and delicateness of this controversy into consideration, we find it hard to imagine why the *News* would not have reconsidered making such a mockery of the situation. The ethics of journalism should never be minimized. Unfortunately, our own school newspaper has demonstrated a fine example of unethical journalism.

Another clear cut bias occurred in the April 14th edition. It seems that much of the *News'* publicity has stemmed from this issue. Why must this controversy always make headline news? By doing this *The Wellesley News* has taken a stand on the whole issue. It would seem that a newspaper should be more perceptive, so as not to let their own personal biases be presented in such a way that they can be taken as truths.

Joy E. Styles '96   Diane Holmes '94
Marisol Rubecindo '96   Nichole R. Phillips '93
Windy Lawrence '96   Thalia V. Shirley '94

Students Confront Andrews on Op-ed
Wellesley News
May 7, 1993

[*Economics professor Marcellus Andrews, though Black, wrote the most anti-Black article spawned by the controversy. He denounced the "student following for a tenured racist," deplored the presence of a "racist Pied Piper" on campus and, most amazingly, endorsed "the judgement of many on the faculty that blacks really are intellectually weak and morally lazy."* – TM]

To the Editor:

Stop and think about the way you view yourself. Are you an individual? Do you weigh all information when it is presented to you? Are you a critical thinker? If you answered yes to these questions, think about the way you would feel if someone made assumptions that stripped you of those qualities and went so far as to publish his opinions for public consumption. Now you will understand, in some small way, why we have decided to confront Marcellus Andrews (and those for whom he was speaking) about his comments in *The Wellesley News*.

While Andrews was "[reflecting] on academic freedom," he took it upon himself to address the problems of young Black people. His decision to grossly generalize the opinions and backgrounds of the women on this campus was wounding. While he would like us to believe that he was referring to a "small number of (mainly) black students," his use of "shallow petit of [sic] bourgeois black collegiate elite" and "little racist clique" to describe one, was enough to cause others of us personal injury. It is very doubtful whether he knows each student about whom he commented well enough to make such assumptions about her mindset and socioeconomic position.

We find it hard to understand why issues surrounding a professor's decision to use *controversial* literature create an opportunity to sling arrows at students. We are not brainwashed little women blindly following the tune of a "racist Pied Piper." We are not so wounded that we would forget what it means to look at all sides of an issue.

Despite the opinions of many people concerning Blacks, we are neither "intellectually weak" nor "morally lazy." Those who think so should confront us on that issue, as well as any other issues that concern us.

No one can *make* us look like fools. Andrews' comment that "young black women are being made to look like fools by someone who pretends to champion the cause of black freedom" is appalling. We have not responded to anything concerning this year's *controversy*. "The events of the past few weeks" that confirm the racist judgements of "many on the faculty," have nothing to do with us. Who are the women taking part in these events and what have they done to be considered fools by people who do not need *events* to occur to confirm their racist views?

In the future, we will take Professor Andrews' advice: we will continue to "finely hone our intellects and our sharp tongues, and use our passions for kicking butt" to let everyone know that the young Black women on this campus are not a group of mindless followers. We are each an intelligent woman and we deserve the right to be recognized as such.

Adriane Williams '96
Thalia Shirley '94
Joy Styles '96
April Towner '95

Diane J. Holmes '94
Cynthia Gibbs '94
April Thomas '96
Kristi Jordan '94

Original Jews Were Africans
Wellesley News
March 3, 1993

I am responding to the articles and an editorial which appeared in the February 19, 1993 issue of the *Wellesley News* regarding the use of the book *The Secret Relationship Between Blacks and Jews* by Professor Tony Martin in his Africana Studies class. The article and editorial question the scholarship of the book (written by the Nation of Islam) and calls the book and its use by Martin anti–Semitic.

Firstly, those who insist upon saying that any African-American is anti–Semitic are not clear on the cultural lineage of Jewish people. The first Jews were Africans – Ethiopians, some of whom set out across Europe thousands of years ago to convert others to their religion. If one were to look up the term "Semitic" in any dictionary, one would find that the term refers to the languages (and by extension the culture) of **Afro-***Asiatic* peoples. *Afro-*means African – most Africans are black. Therefore, **Semitic means black.** For an African-American to be anti-Semitic is for that person to be anti-Black.

Secondly, as to the issue of scholarship. Supposedly, scholarship is based upon rigorous standards set by those who are supposed to be experts in a particular field, in this case Jewish history and the slave trade. However, the standards of scholarship become limiting when applied to African-Americans recounting our own history because they are based upon narrow European perceptions of truth and knowledge – what Europeans deem true is often what is represented as historical and even factual. As has always been the reality, any time Africans and African-Americans attempt to recount their experiences outside the context of Eurocentric scholarship, their accounts are often considered inaccurate.

Finally, if scholarship is based upon factual information, why have facts related to African and African-American history and culture been eliminated from and overlooked in accounts of European and American history? As Professor Martin said in an interview in *The Wellesley News*, one could walk up to any student on this campus and be sure of finding books in their possession which either eliminate the views of Black scholars, do not accurately reflect our glorious history on this planet and/or portray us as negatively as possible. In the interest of fairness, if the above book is to be removed from the curriculum because it is said to promote racism and/or anti-Semitism, then many other books on this campus are guilty of being anti-Black and should be removed from the curriculum at Wellesley as well.

Sincerely,

Dahna M. Chandler
Davis Scholar
Class of '94
Wellesley College

12

An Answer To My Jewish Critics

Being a Speech Delivered to Academic Council
Wellesley College, on March 4, 1993

Truth crushed to earth shall rise again,
The eternal years of God are hers;
But Error, wounded, writhes in pain
And dies among his worshippers.
                    –Bryant

Last week in this august chamber, I had the unique privilege of being a silent witness to what I would describe as a quasi-lynching of myself. I was presumed guilty. I was tried and convicted of heinous crimes, to wit, anti-Semitism. A variety of sentencing options was suggested to the assembled multitude. It did not occur to anybody to solicit my opinion on what was happening, or to seek my perspective on what had transpired. This incredible performance of last week came after about two years of intense attacks on me by my esteemed colleague Mary Lefkowitz in the national media, in the local press, in student publications and via electronic mail transmitted nationally. Lefkowitz, for some time, has had a problem with my class on Africans in Antiquity. She attacked this course in *The New Republic*. She attacked it in *The Chronicle of Higher Education*. In the latter, she described the perspective of Afrocentricity, to which many scholars subscribe, as an irrational development in academia.

The events of last week also came after an unprecedented two weeks of intense attacks upon my character by the *Wellesley News*. For the last three weeks there has been a relentless flood of articles, op eds, editorials and letters to the editor attacking me, accusing me of all kinds of ridiculous crimes. These attacks have been informed by a high level of misinformation, some of it frivolous, much of it scurrilous and most of it mischievous.

To add insult to injury, the very same *Wellesley News* has now declined, on spurious grounds, to publish my response to these offensive attacks, thereby joining the fraternity, or perhaps I should say the sorority, of contemptible rags. The *Wellesley News* has shown itself to be an intolerant and one-sided publication. It has actually exceeded in bigotry the adults whom its youthful editors have sought to emulate. Nevertheless, I will be heard. I insist on being heard. And beginning next week or the week thereafter, at my own expense, I will be publishing a newsletter on this campus which I will endeavour to the best of my ability to circulate. For my perspective must be reckoned with in these proceedings.

President Nan Keohane talked a few minutes ago about differences of opinion and freedom of speech. I would like to discover where in this college that freedom of speech resides. It has certainly not manifested itself over the past two or three weeks.

The Secret Relationship Between Blacks and Jews is a normal, scholarly monograph. Like all scholarly monographs, it focuses on a specific topic, in this case the role that Jews played in the transatlantic slave trade. The book fills in a very important lacuna in our scholarship in this area. For a long time, there have been scattered references to the role of Jews in the slave trade. But this book, for the first time to my knowledge, synthesizes all of this very scattered and difficult to obtain information. Because the people who compiled this book anticipated strident accusations of anti-Semitism, they went to very great lengths to ensure that the overwhelming majority of its sources were derived from Jewish scholarship. I would estimate that perhaps ninety or more percent of the footnotes in this book refer to the work of Jewish historians themselves.

For many years, there have been similar books, articles, and studies dealing with the role of other kinds of people in the slave trade. For the last twenty years, I have myself used readings from a variety of books and articles dealing with the role of Christians in the slave trade. For many years, in fact for my entire twenty years here, I have used readings dealing with the collaborative role of African traitors in the slave trade. I myself was only dimly aware of the Jewish role in African slavery until *The Secret Relationship* was published a couple years or so ago. When I became aware of the role of Jews, I did what I would normally do in any similar situation. I added this new material to my course syllabus.

I am not aware in my twenty years of teaching at Wellesley College that any Christian has objected to the fact that I have highlighted the role of Christians in the slave trade. Nobody has accused me of being anti-Christian. Certainly no African has accused me of being anti-African for mentioning the role of African traitors in selling their own brothers and sisters to the white Jew and Gentile on the West African coast. The question which therefore arises is, what is so special about the Jews that they are beyond the reach of scholarly inquiry?

Before I tell you in more detail what the book does, I will tell you what the book does *not* do. The book does not do what my esteemed colleague and chairman, Selwyn Cudjoe, suggested to Academic Council last week. The book does not suggest that Jews have any particular genetic or other predisposition towards enslaving others. There is no such madness in this book. What the book does do is to document that Jews were heavily invested in the Dutch West India Company, which was a major multinational corporation involved in financing and prosecuting the slave trade, not only to the United States, but also to South America and the Caribbean. *The Secret Relationship* shows that the Jews were a major element in the prosecution of the slave enterprise in places such as Brazil, Curaçao, Suriname, Barbados and Jamaica. Jews were involved in shipping, auctioning and warehousing slaves. Even where they were not heavily involved in plantation agriculture, Jews nevertheless owned and traded slaves.

For the United States of America, the book shows that even though Jews were a relatively small portion of the overall population, they were nevertheless fully involved in the slave trade. Jews participated in every aspect of the peculiar institution. They owned ships that went to Africa and procured slaves. In Newport, Rhode Island, Jews owned every single rum distillery. (Rum distilling was a very important secondary activity around the slave trade.)

Jews in this country were slave traders. They took slaves from one place to the next. Using the research of Jewish historians, the book suggests that based on the 1830 census, Jews actually had a higher per capita slave ownership than for the white population as a whole. The book also suggests that abolitionism was distinguished by a relative scarcity of Jewish voices. Whereas Christians were largely involved in the trade in this country, Christians also were largely the personnel who made up the major white abolitionist societies. The book shows that Jews, like others, resorted to the Bible to rationalize slavery. Pseudo-scientific racism was not confined to Christians. Jews looked at the Bible, among other places, to provide intellectual and moral justification for enslaving Africans.

There is nothing anti-Semitic about this book. I have been passing out, for the last few days, an article from the *New York Amsterdam News*, the largest African American weekly newspaper, which carried a three part series by a Jewish scholar who favorably reviewed the book. So at least there are some Jews who differ from the Jews in this audience who were condemning me last week.

To the Jews, and to their favourite Negroes who have insisted on attacking me I say – one hundred million or more of my people, my ancestors, died in this African slave trade. For nearly five hundred years, Africans in this hemisphere, in the Caribbean, in North, South and Central America were whipped, beaten, brutalized, raped and killed by Jew and Gentile alike. And I say to you, the Jews especially, how dare you! How dare you attempt to tell me, an African descendant of such suffering, that I must put limits on my scholarship, that there must be some limit beyond which my scholarship must not take me. I say that such a suggestion is totally intolerable. Truth crushed to earth shall rise again. The Bible tells us to seek the truth and the truth shall make you free. To those who oppose the truth I say, get out of the way, because the truth is coming at you. Neither the lies and unprincipled attacks of the *Wellesley News,* nor my denial of a hearing by that unfortunate publication, nor the gratuitous *a priori* condemnation emanating from the president and dean, will obscure reality. So do what you want. Do what you feel you have to do. Righteousness will prevail.

The tide of history flows against you.

13

Blacks And Jews At Wellesley News

Broadside No. 1, March 1993   Tony Martin, Ed.
© Copyright 1993, Tony Martin

EDITORIAL STATEMENT

After having been vilified for several weeks in the *Wellesley News* and after having been denied the opportunity to defend myself therein, I now resort to publication of this broadside series, in an effort to let the record reflect more than my detractors' point of view. Issue No. 1 consists solely of my defense of myself, which the *Wellesley News* refused to print. Subsequent issues will deal with other aspects of the controversy surrounding my teaching of *The Secret Relationship Between Blacks and Jews* (Historical Research Department, Nation of Islam, P.O. Box 190551, Boston, MA 02119, $19.95).

The (No Longer) Secret Relationship Between Blacks and Jews

Tony Martin, Africana Studies

The Secret Relationship Between Blacks and Jews (Historical Research Department, Nation of Islam, 1991) is an excellent study of Jewish involvement in the transatlantic slave trade and African slavery. It demonstrates that Jews were very much in the mainstream of European society as far as the trade in African human beings was concerned. While numerous other studies have dealt with the role played by Christians, by African collaborators and by Muslims (especially in relation to the slave trade to Asia), there has hitherto been no effort to synthesize available information on Jewish involvement. This is perhaps surprising, since Jewish domination of the other major transatlantic slave trade has received adequate Jewish coverage – I refer here to "white slavery," the international prostitution of (mainly) Jewish women, by Jewish entrepreneurs in the nineteenth and early twentieth centuries. (See Edward J. Bristow, *Prostitution and Prejudice*).

The Secret Relationship Between Blacks and Jews, using primarily Jewish sources, shows that Jews were fully involved in every aspect of the African slave trade. They were heavily invested in the Dutch West India Company, a multinational corporation (to use modern terminology) specializing in all aspects of the slave trade. They were major slave importers and dealers in places such as Curaçao, Brazil and Barbados. In their Surinamese town of Jew Savannah and elsewhere, they owned substantial numbers of slaves and were zealous participants in European wars waged against slave runaways and maroons. Like their Christian counterparts, they engaged in the full gamut of atrocities visited upon the unfortunate Africans, from whipping to dismembering to rape and murder. In an incident not related in *The Secret Relationship*, J.G. Stedman, a British veteran of Dutch wars against African maroons in Suriname, detailed the story of the African maroon leader Jolly Coeur, who as a young boy was a horrified witness to the rape of his mother by a Jewish slaveowner, one Schults. As an adult Jolly Coeur avenged his mother's rape by flaying Schults, using his skin to keep his powder dry and employing the slaveowner's head to play bowls on the beach. (J.G. Stedman, *Narrative of a Five Years' Expedition Against the Revolted Negroes of Surinam*).

For the United States, *The Secret Relationship* cites U.S. census figures to show that Jews, on a *per capita* basis, often owned more slaves than non-Jews. They owned slave ships that plied the Atlantic and actually owned all the rum distilleries in Newport, R.I. (Rum, distilled from slave-produced molasses, was an important item in the slave trade.)

Jewish abolitionists were few and far between, and the exceptional Jews who opposed slavery were sometimes subjected to the opprobrium of their co-religionists. There is no Jewish counterpart in the United States to the organized Christian abolitionism of the Quakers, Methodists, Baptists and others. Jewish writer (Jonathan Kaufman in *Broken Alliance* admits that

"The Jews who first came to America in the seventeenth, eighteenth, and early nineteenth centuries were heirs to a conservative political tradition that tended to embrace the status quo...." Slavery, of course, was a major part of that status quo.

The Larger Context

The full force of Jewish fury has been unleashed against *The Secret Relationship*. The book has been denounced as "anti-Semitic" and on a par with the greatest racist works of all time. At Wellesley College, the *Wellesley News* has called on students to come forward and testify against it, so that it may be forcibly removed from my syllabus. Wellesley's Academic Council rewarded with polite and prolonged applause the chair of Africana Studies, when, in heart wrenching emotional terms, he, too, denounced the book as "anti-Semitic."

For an explanation of the frenetic response to this quite normal scholarly work, one must look at the history of African American/Jewish relations in the twentieth century. For much of this century, Jews have been a prominent element in the liberal wing of white North America. According to Kaufman, this switch to seeming liberalism (very different from the slavery and earlier post-slavery eras), was facilitated by the development of the Reform Movement in U.S. Judaism in the late nineteenth century, by Jewish involvement in communism and socialism, and by the pursuit of an enlightened Jewish self-interest. In the words of Kaufman, the Jewish "struggle for equality and fair treatment was linked to the struggles of blacks for greater opportunity. It was not a struggle of equals; Jews did not consider their plight equal to that of blacks. But they recognized in the black struggle for rights elements that could benefit them and conditions with which they could sympathize."

Accordingly, several rich and powerful Jews, among them prominent leaders of the U.S. Zionist movement, co-founded, led and financed the National Association for the Advancement of Colored People. (The NAACP, founded in 1909, got its first African American chairperson only in 1975, after the death of chairman Kivie Kaplan, a Boston Jew. The NAACP's highest honor, the Spingarn Medal, is named after one of its early Jewish leaders, Joel

Spingarn.) Jewish influence in African American affairs climaxed in the Civil Rights era of the 1950's and 1960's when, according to Kaufman, three-quarters of the funding raised by the three major Civil Rights organizations (the Student Nonviolent Coordinating Committee, the Congress of Racial Equality and Martin Luther King's Southern Christian Leadership Conference), came from Jewish sources. Jewish influence in the movement was personified by Stanley Levison, one of King's two closest advisors (the other being Andrew Young). Levison drafted King's speeches, handled his finances and served as his chief strategist.

This coalition of unequals came under severe stress after the mid-1960's, when Black Power came to town, emphasizing self-reliance and African American control over their own organizations.

Academia

Jewish influence in African American affairs was reflected also in the realm of scholarship. Jewish scholars came to occupy a powerful position within the area of African American Studies. Names such as Melville Herskovits, Herbert Aptheker, August Meier and a host of others came to be considered by many as the leading authorities on African American history and culture. (The fact that African Americans, unlike Jews, did not own any major publishing companies, doubtless contributed to this state of affairs).

With Black Power came the rise of Black Studies, a greater influx of African Americans into the academic community and a desire for greater control over scholarly interpretations of their own experience. The rise of Afrocentrism and the establishment of African American publishing houses are recent developments in that ongoing struggle.

Jewish Offensive

By the late 1960's the momentum for African American struggle had definitely moved away from the traditional Civil Rights organizations (in which Jews exercised great influence) to the newer groups and individuals favoring a more self-reliant approach to African American struggle. This had serious consequences for Jewish participation in African American affairs. While the powerful NAACP Legal Defense Fund continued under its longstanding Jewish leader, Jack Greenberg, the expulsion of all whites from SNCC and CORE inevitably removed direct Jewish influence from these bodies.

These African American assertions of independence did not sit well with Jews who had grown accustomed to overlordship of the Civil Rights movement, not to mention great influence in the economic life of African American communities. While pockets of Jewish liberalism remained, the dominant Jewish posture was now characterized by the demise of benevolent paternalism and its replacement by an aggressive hostility to continuing African American progress. The new policy brought some impressive Jewish victories, as Jews leveraged off of their great influence within the United States polity, to thwart the rising ambitions of African American folk.

In 1968 Jews defeated the efforts of African Americans in Brooklyn, New York to control the education of their own children, in the Ocean Hill-Brownsville affair. In 1977 the major Jewish organizations intruded themselves as "friends of the court" into the Bakke case, to defeat affirmative action programs for African Americans, Hispanics, Asian Americans and Native Americans. Jews became the major opponents of Jesse Jackson in his two presidential bids. After Minister Louis Farrakhan defended himself against Jewish charges of being an African American Hitler, they raised a hue and cry of "anti-Semitism." The major Jewish publication, *Commentary*, hid behind the first amendment to allow the bigot Arthur Jensen to spew forth his garbage on the supposed genetic inferiority of African Americans. This pseudo-scientific racism reached new heights in 1990 when Jewish City College (New York) professor Michael Levin became the new standard bearer for white supremacy. "On average," he declared, "blacks are significantly less intelligent than whites" (*New York Times*, April 20, 1990). When Nelson Mandela visited New York shortly thereafter, some Jewish elements threatened to disrupt his appearances. Ted Koppel and other Jews on ABC's *Nightline* program (staged at the very same City College), hinted broadly to Mandela that he had better succumb to Jewish pressure or risk losing U.S. support. Mandela had to explain to the Jews that "Your enemies" (in this case Yasir Arafat and the Palestine Liberation Organization) "are not my enemies."

There were many more assaults on African American interests, but perhaps the most memorable was the offensive against Andrew Young. Young was one of the most sacred icons of the African American integrationist, traditionally pro-Jewish establishment. Yet Jewish pressure on President Jimmy Carter cost him his job as U.S. ambassador to the United Nations. His "anti-Semitic" indiscretion consisted of a meeting with a PLO representative. The result was a 1979 summit meeting of the African American political integrationist establishment. Everybody from Coretta Scott King to Jesse Jackson to the NAACP's Benjamin Hooks was there. The Congressional Black Caucus, women's organizations, fraternities and sororities and everyone else deplored the treatment of Andrew Young and issued a "Declaration of Independence" against external control of African American organizations.

The Secret Relationship and Wellesley College

The Jewish scholar Nathan Glazer sought to provide intellectual justification for this onslaught. In his *Affirmative Discrimination* (1975) he turned history upside down to argue that white ethnic groups (such as Jews) who had arrived "post-1880" (as if no Jews had arrived before 1880), "were not particularly involved in the enslavement of the Negro or the creation of the Jim Crow pattern in the South...or the near extermination of the American Indian....There is little reason for them to feel that they should bear the burden of redressing a past in which they had no or little part...." B'nai B'rith repeated these falsehoods in its brief for the Bakke case.

This falsification of history is now corrected by *The Secret Relationship Between Blacks and Jews*, which documents Jewish involvement, not only in African slavery but in the extermination of the Native Americans as well. The predominant Jewish response has been, all too predictably, to denounce the book and all who use it (myself included), as "anti-Semitic." "Anti-Semitism," once presumably the anguished cry of an oppressed people, has become, for the privileged and powerful U.S. Jewish leadership and their unthinking Negro stooges, a bludgeon to subdue dissent, stifle discussion, deprive African Americans of a living and perpetuate historical lies.

"Anti-Semitism" has also become a clever smokescreen for a burgeoning Jewish intolerance of truly Stalinist proportions. Last year my esteemed Wellesley College colleague Mary Lefkowitz, Andrew Mellon professor (the same one who did not know that Herodotus had referred to the doctrine of the immortality of the soul; the same one who recently insulted our Martin Luther King, Jr. memorial speaker, Dr. Yosef ben-Jochannon, in the college chapel), launched into a sudden and unprovoked attack on my "Africans in Antiquity" course. She became displeased at the suggestion that Africans had pioneered civilization and influenced Ancient Greece.

She took the unprecedented step of intriguing with the dean of the college to rewrite the description of my course in the preliminary college catalog, without my knowledge or consent. She also attacked the course in the conservative Jewish-owned *New Republic* and in the *Chronicle of Higher Education,* where she described Afrocentrism as an irrational development. (Neither publication allowed me to respond). Several years earlier the resident Jewish Studies expert in Wellesley's Religion department had written the Curriculum Committee in an unsuccessful attempt to prevent me from teaching this course at all. On February 21, 1993, two days after my return from a lecture engagement at Gettysburg College, Lefkowitz despatched a memo to contacts there warning them against Afrocentric scholars in general and Dr. ben-Jochannon in particular. "It seems to me," she wrote, "that the promulgation on college campuses of this type of 'information' is a very great danger to our subject, since it is often delivered to students in contexts where no competent historian of the ancient world is welcome or able to be present." And now I learn from the *Wellesley News* that Hillel students not registered in my African American survey course sat in, unknown to me, in order to monitor my references to *The Secret Relationship Between Blacks and Jews.*

This type of mindless intolerance is clearly not acceptable. Despite their recent victories, Jews have nothing to gain in the long run from picking fights with an aroused and conscious African American population. They must realize that slavery has ended. It ended some time ago. And even though some handkerchief heads will always be among us, the cozy paternalism of the Civil Rights era has run its course. It is not too late to reverse the current trends, but any rapprochement between African Americans and Jews will have to be predicated on mutual respect. And mutual respect will entail reparations from both Jew and Gentile for four centuries of unrequited toil. Nathan Glazer argued that "Compensation for the past is a dangerous principle," but it is unlikely that he found fault with the billions in reparations paid by Germany to the Jewish state of Israel. The day of Africa's reparations must come.

Index

ABC, 14, 16, 74, 133
academic council, x, 9, 16, 38, 40, 119, 125, 127, 131
Adelman, Ken, 74
Adelson, "Prof." Howard L., 28-29, 30, 32, 37, 54-56, 63, 64, 71
Adkins, LaTrese, x, 118
ADL. *See* Anti-Defamation League
Affirmative Discrimination (Glazer), 134
African American-African summit, 24
African Black Students Organization of San Francisco State University, 46
African Fundamentalism (Garvey), 51
African National Congress, 46, 74
African Nationalist Construction Movement, 41
African National Reparations Organization, 46
Africans in Antiquity, 59, 135
Afro-Canadian, The, 87, 91
Afrocentrism, 51-66; defined, 51
AIPAC. *See* American Israel Public Affairs Committee
Akbar, Dr. Na'im, *Visions for Black Men*, 103
Alcmene, 63
Ali, Noble Drew, 103
All-African Peoples Revolutionary Party, 46
Amasis, 62
American Academy of Arts and Sciences, 21
American Book Award, 21
American Federation of Labour, 72
American Israel Public Affairs Committee, 4, 39, 100, 106
American Jewish Committee, 8, 9, 15, 20, 30, 31, 38, 52, 53, 54, 71, 72, 76, 110, 114, 117; libelous press release, 8-12
American Jewish Congress, 8, 74, 109, 117; libelous press release, 8-12
American Library Association, 107
American Muslim Mission, 46
American Publishers Association, 21
Ammon, 61, 63
Amphitryon, 63
Amsterdam News, 33, 47, 110, 128

Andrews, Marcellus, 9, 28, 32, 121, 122; anti-Black statement of, 19-20; attacked by students, 121; attacks Black women, 19-20; compared with Uncle Tom, 20
Andromeda, 61
Annual Conference of Ethnic Communities, 71
Anti-Defamation League, 3, 6, 8, 10, 11, 19, 21, 29, 33, 38, 43, 44, 46, 47, 48, 49, 52, 68, 74, 75, 100, 109, 112, 114, 115, 117; as a "Defamation League", 11; libelous diatribes of, 10; libelous press release, 8-12; organizations targeted by, 46; spy operation of, 46
Antony and Cleopatra (Shakespeare), 59
Aptheker, Herbert, 132
Arafat, Yasir, 74, 134
Argos, 61
Aryan model, 64
Asante, Dr. Molefi, ix, 59
Asantewa, Yaa, 94
Ashkenazi Jews, 111
Associated Press, 13

B'nai B'rith, 3, 106, 134
Babylon, 61
Bakke case, 23, 43, 55, 133, 134
Barbados, 90, 112, 127, 130
Begin, Menachem, 54
ben-Jochannon, Dr.Yosef, 6, 7, 58, 59, 102, 135
Benin, 65
Bernal, Martin, 58, 59, 64, 65, 66; *Black Athena*, 57, 66; denounces Afrocentrism, 64
Bertley, Dr. Leo W., ix, 87
Bible, 98, 128
Birch, John, 31
Black American Leadership Meeting, 22-25
Black Athena (Bernal), 57, 58, 66
Black Books Revolution, 42
Black Consciousness Movement of Azania, 46
Black Life, 70
Black Power, 77, 132

137

Books from the Majority Press

THE NEW MARCUS GARVEY LIBRARY

Literary Garveyism: Garvey, Black Arts and the Harlem Renaissance. Tony Martin. $19.95 (cloth), $9.95 (paper).

The Poetical Works of Marcus Garvey. Tony Martin, Ed. $17.95 (cloth), $9.95 (paper).

Marcus Garvey, Hero: A First Biography. Tony Martin. $19.95 (cloth), $8.95 (paper).

The Pan-African Connection. Tony Martin. $22.95 (cloth), $10.95 (paper).

Message to the People: The Course of African Philosophy. Marcus Garvey. Ed. by Tony Martin. $22.95 (cloth), $9.95 (paper).

Race First: The Ideological and Organizational Struggles of Marcus Garvey and the Universal Negro Improvement Association. Tony Martin. $12.95 (paper).

The Philosophy and Opinions of Marcus Garvey. Amy Jacques Garvey, Ed. $12.95 (paper).

Amy Ashwood Garvey: Pan-Africanist, Feminist and Wife No. 1. Tony Martin. Forthcoming 1994.

African Fundamentalism: A Literary and Cultural Anthology of Garvey's Harlem Renaissance. Tony Martin, Ed. $14.95 (paper).

THE BLACK WORLD

Brazil: Mixture or Massacre? Essays in the Genocide of a Black People. Abdias do Nascimento. $12.95 (paper).

Studies in the African Diaspora: A Memorial to James R. Hooker (1929-1976). John P. Henderson and Harry A. Reed, Eds. $39.95 (cloth).

In Nobody's Backyard: The Grenada Revolution in its Own Words. Vol. I, the Revolution at Home. Tony Martin, Ed. $22.95 (cloth). **Vol. II, Facing the World.** Tony Martin, Ed. $22.95 (cloth).

Guinea's Other Suns: The African Dynamic in Trinidad Culture. Maureen Warner-Lewis. $9.95 (paper).

Carlos Cooks: And Black Nationalism from Garvey to Malcolm. Robert, Nyota and Grandassa Harris, Eds. $9.95 (paper).

From Kingston to Kenya: The Making of a Pan-Africanist Lawyer. Dudley Thompson, with Margaret Cezair Thompson. $10.95 (paper).

The Jewish Onslaught: Despatches from the Wellesley Battlefront. Tony Martin. $9.95 (paper).

The Afro-Trinidadian: Endangered Species/Oh, What a Nation! Tony Martin. Forthcoming 1994.

Order from The Majority Press, P.O. Box 538, Dover, MA 02030, U.S.A.
Mass. residents add 5% sales tax.